# Somatic Therapy Workbook

## Release Trauma Stored in the Body, Recover From Complex PTSD, Relieve Stress, and Regulate Your Nervous System

Rachel Singer

# Table of Contents

# About Me and Why I Wrote This Book

I was thirty the first time I realized my body was keeping score.

I'd been sitting in my therapist's office for months, talking through everything I could think of. My childhood. My relationships. The decisions that led me to feel so chronically anxious I couldn't sleep through the night. We'd circle the same stories week after week, and I'd leave feeling temporarily lighter, like I'd confessed something important. By the next morning, though, my chest would tighten again. My jaw would clench. The knot in my stomach would return like clockwork.

One afternoon, mid-session, my therapist asked me to pause. "Where do you feel that right now?" she said. "In your body, I mean."

I looked at her blankly. I had no idea what she was talking about.

She asked me to close my eyes and notice what was happening physically while I spoke. I tried. Nothing came. I couldn't feel anything except a vague sense of discomfort I'd learned to ignore years ago. It was like trying to read a language I'd never been taught.

That moment cracked something open. I started to understand that all the talking in the world wasn't going to reach the part of me that was still holding on. My nervous system had its own memory, its own logic, and it wasn't interested in the narratives I'd built to make sense of my pain. It was operating on a different frequency entirely.

That realization didn't fix anything right away. If anything, it made things harder. I had to learn a completely new way of listening to myself. I had to stop treating my body like a machine that occasionally malfunctioned and start seeing it as the place where my actual experience lived. The panic attacks, the chronic tension in my shoulders, the way I'd freeze when someone raised their voice: none of it was random. It was all information. My body had been trying to tell me something for years, and I'd spent all that time trying to think my way out of it instead.

I started exploring somatic therapy, nervous system work, anything that addressed what was happening below the surface of my thoughts. I read everything I could find. Some of it helped. A lot of it didn't. The books that were research-heavy felt inaccessible. The ones that promised quick fixes felt dishonest. I wanted something that met me where I actually was: confused, scared, willing to try, but exhausted by the idea that healing required me to be anything other than exactly what I was in that moment.

It took years of fumbling through different approaches before I found what worked. I learned about polyvagal theory and why my body would shut down in moments of stress. I discovered Internal Family Systems and started recognizing the different parts of myself that had been fighting for control. I worked with somatic practitioners who taught me that healing didn't have to mean reliving everything. Sometimes, the body just needed permission to release what it had been holding.

I also learned that this work isn't linear. There were weeks I felt like I'd made real progress, and then something small would trigger me and I'd be right back where I started. I'd get frustrated with myself for not "getting better" fast enough. I'd compare my healing to other people's and feel like I was doing it wrong. It took a long time to accept that healing looks different for everyone, and that there's no timeline you're supposed to follow.

The truth is, even now at forty-three, I'm still figuring parts of this out. I still have days when my nervous system gets hijacked by something I thought I'd processed. I still catch myself holding my breath when I'm stressed, or realize I've been clenching my jaw for hours without noticing. The difference now is that I know what's happening. I can work with it instead of against it.

I'm not a therapist. I'm not a researcher. I don't have letters after my name or a practice where I see clients. What I have is my own experience, and the understanding that came from living through it. Over the past thirteen years, I've had the privilege of time: time to read, to learn, to piece together what actually helped and what was just noise. I spent years translating clinical concepts into language that made sense to me, testing exercises that felt genuine instead of performative, and figuring out how to integrate this work into daily life without turning it into another thing I could fail at.

Outside of this work, I'm pretty ordinary. I drink too much coffee. I take long walks when I need to think. I have a tendency to start too many projects at once and then get overwhelmed by all of them. I'm not someone who has it all figured out. I'm just someone who's been doing this work long enough to know what helped me, and what might help you too.

I wrote this book because I needed it years ago and it didn't exist. Not in the form I needed, anyway. I needed something practical but not prescriptive. Something that acknowledged how hard this work is without making it feel impossible. Something that trusted me to know my own body, even when I didn't feel like I did.

I also wrote it because I believe talking about trauma shouldn't require us to perform recovery in a certain way. You don't have to have everything figured out to begin. You don't have to pretend you're doing better than you are. You just have to be willing to start paying attention differently.

This book is about giving you tools to work with what your body already knows. It's about building safety from the inside out, and learning to trust that your nervous system isn't working against you. It's been trying to protect you all along, even when it doesn't feel that way.

If any part of what I've shared here sounds familiar, if you've ever felt disconnected from your body, or stuck in patterns you can't think your way out of, or frustrated that traditional therapy wasn't enough, this book is for you. Not because I have all the answers, but because I've been where you are. And I know that starting is the hardest part.

So let's start together.

# Introduction

*"The body says what words cannot."* — Martha Graham

You've tried talking about it. You've gone to therapy, maybe for months or years. You've worked to understand where your anxiety comes from, why you shut down in certain situations, why your body reacts before your mind can catch up. You've gained insight. You can name your triggers. You can explain your patterns to someone who asks.

And still, something hasn't shifted.

Your chest still tightens when you walk into a crowded room. Your shoulders still carry tension you can't release. You still freeze when someone raises their voice, even when you know you're safe. You've done the cognitive work, but your body hasn't gotten the message. It's still operating like the danger never ended.

That's not because you're doing something wrong. It's because trauma doesn't live in your thoughts. It lives in your nervous system, in the tissues that learned to brace for impact, in the patterns your body created to survive. Talk therapy reaches your mind. This workbook reaches the place where trauma actually lives.

This isn't about replacing therapy or dismissing what you've already done. It's about adding the piece that's been missing. Somatic work meets you where words can't go. It teaches your body what your mind already knows: that you're safe now, that you can let go, that the threat has passed.

The exercises in this book are simple, but they're not easy. They ask you to pay attention in ways you've learned to avoid. They invite you to feel what you've spent years trying not to feel. They require patience, gentleness, and the willingness to move at your own pace. There's no timeline here. No pressure to be further along than you are. Healing happens in the body's time, not the calendar's.

Each chapter builds on the one before it, but you don't have to follow them in order if something else calls to you first. Trust your instincts. Your body knows what it needs, even when your mind isn't sure. If a chapter feels too activating, skip it and come back later. If an exercise brings up more than you can handle alone, pause and reach out for support. This work is meant to help, not overwhelm.

You'll find tools here for building safety, reconnecting with your body, working with dissociation, releasing trapped emotions, understanding chronic pain, and regulating your nervous system. You'll learn about Internal Family Systems and how different parts of you have been trying to protect you all along. You'll discover practices you can use when anxiety spikes, when you feel numb, when the world feels like too much.

Some days, the tools will work. Other days, they won't. That's normal. Healing isn't linear. You'll have breakthroughs and setbacks, moments of clarity and stretches where everything feels stuck. All of it is part of the process. Keep going anyway.

This book won't fix everything. It won't erase what happened or make trauma disappear. What it can do is give you ways to work with your body instead of against it, to listen to what it's been trying to tell you, to build a relationship with your nervous system that feels less like a battle and more like a partnership.

If you're reading this, you've already taken the hardest step. You've acknowledged that something needs to change, and you've decided to try. That takes courage. It takes willingness. It takes showing up for yourself even when you're not sure it will help.

So start here. Start small. Start with one exercise, one breath, one moment of noticing. Your body has been waiting for you to come back. It's ready when you are.

## Setting Your Intention

Before you begin this work, take a moment to acknowledge why you're here. Not what you think you should want, but what you actually hope for. Maybe it's relief. Maybe it's understanding. Maybe it's just the ability to get through a day without your body feeling like a threat.

There's no right answer. Whatever brought you to this book is enough.

*What I hope to find in this work:*

________________________________________

________________________________________

________________________________________

*One thing I'm willing to try, even if it feels uncomfortable:*

________________________________________

________________________________________

*How I'll know this work is helping (what might feel different in my body or my life):*

________________________________________

________________________________________

________________________________________

You can return to this page anytime. Your intention might shift as you move through the book, and that's okay. Let it evolve. Let yourself change. That's what healing looks like.

# Chapter 1:
# Your Body Holds the Story Your Mind Forgot

*"The body keeps the score." — Bessel van der Kolk*

Sarah sits across from her therapist, recounting a childhood incident with remarkable composure. Her words are measured, her narrative coherent. She's told this story before, many times. She understands the impact it had on her developing sense of self. She can identify the cognitive distortions it created. She's done the work.

But her body tells a different story.

Her hands grip the chair's armrests, knuckles white. Her jaw clenches and releases in a rhythm she doesn't notice. Her breathing stays shallow, trapped in her upper chest. When the therapist gently points this out, Sarah looks down at her hands with genuine surprise. She hadn't felt any of it.

You might tell a hard story cleanly, while your hands, jaw, and breath report something you didn't notice.

This disconnect between what we know and what we feel, between our understanding and our experience, is where many of us live after trauma. We can articulate what happened. We can analyze patterns, identify triggers, and intellectually grasp how our past shaped our present. Yet something remains untouched. The racing heart when someone raises their voice. The inexplicable exhaustion that no amount of sleep fixes. The sense of danger that arrives without warning, flooding our system before our mind can catch up.

If you've done therapy and still feel stuck, you're not failing. If you understand your trauma but can't seem to move past it, you're not broken. If talking about what happened has helped you make sense of your story but hasn't freed you from its grip, you're discovering something essential: trauma doesn't just live in your memories or thoughts. It lives in your tissues, your nervous system, the very cells that make up your body.

Your body has been holding what your mind learned to forget. The tension you carry signals unfinished protection. Numbness reads as survival. The hypervigilance that exhausts you is a nervous system that never got the message that the danger has passed.

This workbook starts from a different premise than traditional approaches to healing. It begins with the recognition that your body isn't just carrying symptoms of trauma. It's actively trying to complete responses that got interrupted, to finish what couldn't be finished when you were overwhelmed. Your physical symptoms are communications to understand, messengers carrying information about what still needs to happen for you to feel safe again.

You're here to listen to what your body has been saying all along.

## Why Talk Therapy Alone Isn't Enough for Trauma

When Emma first started therapy at 28, she felt hopeful. Finally, someone who could help her understand why she felt so anxious, why relationships felt impossible, why she startled at sudden movements and couldn't relax even on vacation. She talked about her childhood: the unpredictability, the walking on eggshells, the moments that taught her the world wasn't safe. Her therapist was compassionate and skilled. They worked through cognitive patterns, identified her triggers, developed coping strategies.

Three years later, Emma could explain her trauma with eloquence. She understood how her hypervigilance developed, why she struggled with trust, how her childhood shaped her nervous system. But understanding hadn't changed one fundamental thing: she still woke up at 3 a.m. with her heart pounding. She still felt her chest tighten when her partner's tone shifted. She still left social gatherings feeling like she'd run a marathon, her body buzzing with an exhaustion that went deeper than tired.

You can describe the pattern and still wake at 3 a.m. with your heart sprinting.

"I feel like I've talked about it to death," she told a friend. "I know everything about why I'm like this. So why do I still feel this way?"

Emma's experience points to something that trauma researchers have spent decades trying to help us understand: knowing about trauma and healing from trauma are two different things.

Traditional talk therapy operates primarily in the realm of language, narrative, and conscious thought. When you sit with a therapist and talk about what happened, you're engaging the thinking part of your brain where you process information, make sense of experiences, create meaning from chaos, and develop insight. Talk therapy can be powerful for this work. It helps you understand patterns, challenge unhelpful beliefs, and reframe your story in ways that feel less overwhelming.

But trauma doesn't live primarily in this thinking, talking part of your brain.

When something traumatic happens, your body responds instantly: heart rate spikes, muscles tense, stress hormones flood your system, blood flows away from your digestive system and toward your limbs so you can fight or flee. These responses happen in milliseconds, far faster than conscious thought. They're designed to save your life, not to be reasonable or proportional.

During repeated trauma, especially in childhood, these survival responses get encoded at a level that exists below language. The imprint lives in implicit memory: the kind of memory that shapes how your body responds to the world without conscious recollection. You might not remember specific incidents (especially if you were very young), but your body remembers. It remembers in the form of tension patterns, startle responses, digestive issues, chronic pain, and a nervous system calibrated to expect danger.

When a door slams, your shoulders jump before a thought forms. That jump needs attention more than the explanation.

Talk therapy helps you name the story and build understanding; somatic work lets your body complete what survival began. For many people, talking is an essential part of healing, helping you create a coherent narrative, understand your reactions, and develop new ways of thinking about yourself. But for Complex Post-Traumatic Stress Disorder (Complex PTSD), where trauma is stored not just in memory but in the body's threat response system, talking alone often can't reach the places that need healing most.

Your body learned to protect you through physical responses: bracing, numbing, hypervigilance, shutdown. Healing needs to speak the body's language too.

---

### EXERCISE: Where Talk Therapy Stopped

---

This exercise helps you identify what remains unresolved in your body, even after therapeutic work.

Complete the following reflections:

*One thing I intellectually understand about my trauma:*

________________________________________________________________

________________________________________________________________

*One physical symptom or body sensation that persists despite this understanding:*

________________________________________________________________

________________________________________________________________

*When this physical symptom shows up, my body feels:*

________________________________________________________________

________________________________________________________________

*If this sensation could speak, it might be saying:*

________________________________________________________________

________________________________________________________________

*Notes: Place a star next to the one body cue that shows up most often.*

________________________________________________________________

## What Happens When Trauma Gets Trapped in Your Body

Picture a deer grazing in a meadow. A predator appears. Instantly, the deer's entire system mobilizes: adrenaline surges, muscles tense, heart pounds. The deer bolts, running with everything it has. Let's say the deer escapes. Once safe, something remarkable happens: the deer's body trembles and shakes, sometimes for several minutes. This isn't fear. It's the deer's nervous system discharging the massive amount of survival energy that mobilized for escape. After this shaking completes, the deer returns to grazing, calm, as if nothing happened. The threat has passed, and the body knows it.

Your body is designed to do something similar. When you face danger, your nervous system mobilizes huge amounts of energy to help you fight or flee. Your muscles tense to spring into action. Your heart pounds to pump blood to your limbs. Stress hormones flood your system to give you strength and speed. This is your body's brilliant survival response, honed over millions of years of evolution.

But here's where human trauma gets complicated.

When you're a child living with unpredictable rage, you can't fight back. You can't flee; you depend on the very people who frighten you. When you face ongoing threat with no escape, when you're overpowered or trapped, when social rules prevent you from responding, your body mobilizes for action but has nowhere to go. The energy meant for fighting or fleeing gets locked inside. Your muscles tense for a battle that never comes, or they freeze when movement would have brought more danger.

Unlike the deer, you don't get to shake and tremble until the stress discharges. You might have been told to calm down, stop crying, or pull yourself together. You might have learned that showing fear made things worse. You might have needed to go straight from a terrifying incident to sitting quietly at the dinner table or doing homework. The fight that couldn't happen, the flight that was impossible, the scream that had to be swallowed stays in your system.

The cycle started in your body never finished.

Years later, your shoulders might stay perpetually raised, braced for impact that isn't coming. Your jaw might clench so habitually you don't notice until someone points out you grind your teeth in your sleep. Your stomach might churn with anxiety that has no obvious source, because your digestive system learned to stay in emergency mode. Your muscles might ache with tension that never releases, or you might feel exhausted for no clear reason: the result of a nervous system that's been in high alert so long it's running on empty.

Some people carry this as always scanning for danger, jumping at sounds, unable to relax even in safe environments. Your body stays ready for the next threat, muscles slightly tensed, breath shallow, always prepared to react. You might feel wired, restless, like you're running on nervous energy that never quite burns out.

Others experience numbness, disconnection, a feeling of being cut off from your body. When your nervous system becomes overwhelmed by activation it couldn't discharge, it essentially shuts down to protect you. You might feel spacey, foggy, like you're watching your life from behind glass. Physical sensations feel distant or absent. When you couldn't fight or flee, your nervous system did the only thing left: it took you offline so you wouldn't have to feel the full impact of what was happening.

Your body might alternate between these states. Periods of anxious hyperarousal followed by crashes into numbness and exhaustion. Or you might live primarily in one state (either revved up or shut down) with occasional flips to the other side when something triggers a different response, then a long exhale you didn't notice you were holding.

These aren't random symptoms. Your body is still holding defensive responses that never got to complete. The tension is your body still bracing against danger. The numbness is your body still protecting you from overwhelm. Your threat detection system is still working overtime because it never received the all-clear signal.

Healing means helping your body finally complete what it started: discharging the survival energy that got stuck, allowing your nervous system to recognize that the danger has passed, that it's safe enough now to let go of defenses you needed then but don't need anymore.

---

### EXERCISE: Body Symptoms Inventory

---

This checklist helps you identify physical patterns that may be related to trapped trauma responses.

Check any symptoms you experience regularly (at least once a week):

**Muscular & Skeletal:**

- ☐ Chronic neck or shoulder tension
- ☐ Lower back pain without clear injury
- ☐ Jaw clenching or teeth grinding
- ☐ Headaches or migraines
- ☐ General muscle aches or stiffness
- ☐ Widespread, migrating pain

**Digestive & Internal:**

- ☐ Stomach aches or nausea
- ☐ Irritable bowel symptoms
- ☐ Difficulty swallowing or lump in throat
- ☐ Chest tightness or pain
- ☐ Chronic fatigue despite rest
- ☐ Immune system issues (frequent illness)

**Nervous System:**

- ☐ Jumpiness or exaggerated startle response
- ☐ Restlessness or inability to sit still
- ☐ Feeling "wired" or anxious without cause
- ☐ Difficulty falling or staying asleep
- ☐ Racing heart or palpitations
- ☐ Feeling spacey, foggy, or disconnected

**Sensory & Breathing:**

- ☐ Shallow breathing or breath holding
- ☐ Dizziness or lightheadedness
- ☐ Temperature regulation issues (cold hands/feet)
- ☐ Numbness or tingling in extremities
- ☐ Feeling "not quite in your body"
- ☐ Difficulty sensing hunger, fullness, or pain

**Patterns I notice:**

*When these symptoms are strongest:*

------------------------------------------------------------------------

*Body areas that hold the most tension:*

------------------------------------------------------------------------

***Notes:*** *Choose no more than three symptoms to track this week.*

## The Science Behind Somatic Healing

Billions of connections in your brain determine how you think, feel, and respond to the world. For most of human history, scientists believed that once your brain finished developing in early adulthood, these pathways were essentially fixed. The architecture of your brain, for better or worse, was permanent.

Then neuroscience discovered neuroplasticity.

Neuroplasticity is your brain's ability to rewire itself throughout your entire life. Every time you learn something new, have a different experience, or practice a new behavior, you're physically changing your brain. Neurons that fire together wire together, creating stronger connections. Pathways you stop using eventually weaken and fade. Your brain is constantly reshaping itself based on what you do, think, and practice.

This discovery changed everything we know about healing from trauma.

The neural pathways that trauma carved into your brain (the ones that make you startle at loud noises, feel unsafe in your own home, or automatically brace against criticism) aren't permanent. They feel permanent because they've been reinforced thousands of times. Every time your body responds to a perceived threat the same way, that pathway gets stronger. But neuroplasticity means you can build new pathways. You can literally rewire your brain's response to the world.

Here's what makes somatic healing particularly powerful: it works from the bottom up.

Your brain has three main layers. At the top sits your cortex: the thinking, reasoning part where language and conscious thought happen. This is what you engage in traditional talk therapy. Below that lies your limbic system, which handles emotions and memory. At the base sits your brainstem and nervous system: the most primitive part that governs survival responses, operates below conscious awareness, and controls your body's automatic functions like breathing, heart rate, and threat detection.

Complex PTSD gets encoded at this deepest level. When your body learned that the world was dangerous, when your nervous system calibrated itself to expect threat, those lessons were written into your brainstem and autonomic nervous system: areas that don't speak in words and don't respond to logic.

Bottom-up approaches like somatic healing work directly with this layer. Instead of trying to think your way out of trauma, you work with the body's sensations, movement, and nervous system states. You're speaking the language of the part of your brain where trauma actually lives.

This is where the vagus nerve becomes important. This remarkable nerve is the main communication highway between your brain and body, carrying signals in both directions. About 80% of its fibers run from body to brain, meaning your brain is constantly receiving information about what's happening in your body, information that shapes your emotional state and sense of safety before conscious thought gets involved.

When your body is tense, your vagus nerve sends signals that reinforce the sense of danger. When your breathing is shallow, your brain receives information consistent with threat. Your body's state directly influences your emotional and cognitive experience. You can know intellectually that you're safe while your body is sending stronger signals that say otherwise.

Somatic healing works with this communication system. When you learn to shift your body's state (releasing chronic tension, deepening your breath, allowing incomplete defensive responses to complete), you change the signals traveling through your vagus nerve to your brain. You're giving your brain new information about safety. You're creating felt experiences of calm, rather than just thinking about calm.

You can work with sensations even without explicit memory. You don't need to analyze or understand every trigger. You don't need your thinking brain to convince your survival brain that it's overreacting. Instead, you work directly with the sensations and responses in your body, allowing your nervous system to gradually learn, through experience rather than explanation, that the danger has passed.

Studies of somatic approaches like Somatic Experiencing, Sensorimotor Psychotherapy, and trauma-sensitive yoga report shifts in startle, numbness, and baseline arousal that cognitive work often doesn't touch. These changes show up particularly in symptoms like hypervigilance, emotional disconnection, and the physiological activation that keeps trauma alive in the present moment.

Your body wants to heal. It's been trying to complete these interrupted responses, to discharge this stuck energy, to return to a state of ease. Somatic healing creates the conditions where it can finally happen. You're working with your body's innate wisdom, not against it.

The changes might feel subtle at first. A moment where your shoulders drop and you take a full breath. A situation that usually triggers you but this time feels slightly less overwhelming. An increasing ability to sense what's happening in your body rather than being cut off from it. These small shifts are your nervous system beginning to rewire, creating new pathways that will get stronger each time you practice.

When your breath drops lower and your eyes soften, your brain gets new information to wire around.

---

### EXERCISE: Your First Body Check-In

---

This brief practice introduces gentle body awareness without trying to change anything.

1. Find a comfortable position, either sitting or standing. You can keep your eyes open with a soft gaze or close them if that feels safe.
2. Take a moment to notice your breath, wherever you feel it most easily: maybe at your nostrils, your chest, or your belly. You're not trying to change your breathing, just noticing it as it is right now.
3. Now bring your attention to your heartbeat. You might feel it in your chest, your throat, or your wrists. Can you sense it? Don't worry if you can't; simply noticing that you're trying is enough.
4. Finally, feel your feet on the ground or your body in the chair. Notice the sensation of contact, of being supported by something solid beneath you.

That's it. You've just completed your first somatic check-in.

*What I noticed:*

______________________________________________________________________________

______________________________________________________________________________

______________________________________________________________________________

**Notes:** Write one sentence about where you felt the heartbeat most clearly.

______________________________________________________________________________

## Understanding Your Nervous System as Your Survival Alarm

Imagine a smoke detector in your home. Its job is simple: detect smoke and sound the alarm. It can't tell the difference between danger and annoyance. It just does what it's designed to do: alert you to potential threat so you can respond.

Your nervous system works the same way, but instead of smoke, it's constantly scanning for signs of danger or safety. This process (called neuroception) happens completely outside your conscious awareness. Before you can think about whether something is threatening, your nervous system has already detected cues in your environment and begun responding.

When neuroception detects safety, your nervous system settles into what's called ventral vagal state: the social engagement system. In this state, your face is relaxed, your voice has natural prosody, you can make eye contact comfortably, and you feel curious, open, and connected to others. This is the state where healing happens, where you can learn and grow, where relationships feel possible. In ventral, you catch a friend's expression and feel your chest widen.

When neuroception detects danger, your nervous system shifts into sympathetic activation: the fight-or-flight response. Your heart rate increases, your muscles tense, your breath quickens. You feel agitated, anxious, angry, or panicked. You might talk faster, feel restless, or experience an urge to escape. Your body is mobilizing energy to deal with a threat. A work email late at night sends your pulse climbing.

When neuroception detects life threat (a situation where neither fighting nor fleeing seems possible), your nervous system drops into dorsal vagal shutdown. This is the freeze or collapse response. Your heart rate may slow, your muscles go limp, you might feel numb or foggy, disconnected from your body and emotions. Time might seem to slow down or speed up. You're still conscious, but you've essentially gone offline to conserve energy and minimize pain. Your partner's silence drops you into fog and distance.

These shifts happen before thought. They're automatic responses controlled by your autonomic nervous system, which operates far faster than conscious awareness.

Here's what makes Complex PTSD so exhausting: your nervous system's smoke detector got recalibrated.

If you live with Complex PTSD, your nervous system learned that the world isn't safe. In chronic unpredictability, your detector learns to fire early. That fast alarm kept you safe; now it rings for burnt toast. If you needed to detect the subtle shift in your parent's voice that signaled danger, or read micro-expressions to know when to make yourself invisible, your threat detection system became incredibly attuned. This heightened sensitivity kept you safe when you were young and vulnerable.

But now that sensitivity remains. Your nervous system reads neutral cues as dangerous ones. A coworker's neutral tone sounds angry. A partner's thoughtful silence feels like rejection. A change in plans feels catastrophic. The same sensitivity that protected you then keeps you trapped in survival states now.

You might live most of your time in sympathetic activation: always on edge, ready for the next crisis, unable to truly rest even when nothing is wrong. Or you might spend long periods in shutdown: disconnected, numb, going through the motions but not really present. Many people with Complex PTSD flip between these states: anxious and hypervigilant one day, collapsed and exhausted the next, rarely spending time in the green zone of social engagement where life feels manageable.

Your system learned to protect you in the quickest way it knew. It learned that the world requires constant vigilance. It never learned what safety actually feels like, or if it did, those experiences weren't frequent or reliable enough to become the default expectation.

When your therapist suggests you "just relax" or someone tells you there's nothing to worry about, they're speaking to your thinking brain. But your nervous system isn't listening to thoughts. It's responding to felt experience, to patterns it learned years ago, to a baseline expectation that the world is fundamentally unsafe.

You can know intellectually that you're safe while your body screams otherwise. You can understand that your partner's silence isn't threatening while your heart races and your hands shake. The thinking part of your brain and the survival part of your nervous system are operating on different information.

Your nervous system isn't trying to make your life difficult. It's trying to protect you. Every anxiety spike, every moment of numbness, every time you react in ways that seem out of proportion to the actual situation, your system believes it's keeping you safe based on the training it received.

Healing means helping your nervous system learn something new through repeated experiences of actual safety: moments where your body can begin to recognize that the danger has passed, that you can let down your guard without catastrophe, that there are people and places where threat detection can soften.

You're creating conditions where your system can gradually recalibrate itself, where the smoke detector can become less sensitive because the environment has genuinely changed.

You'll stack short, repeatable moments where your body recognizes safe enough.

---

### ✎ EXERCISE: Recognizing Your Alarm States

---

This tracking exercise helps you identify when your nervous system shifts between states, building awareness without judgment.

Over the next few days, notice moments when you recognize your nervous system activating. Use this simple framework:

**Sympathetic Activation (fight-or-flight)** feels like:

- Racing thoughts or heart
- Muscle tension, jaw clenching
- Agitation, irritability, or panic
- Urge to move, escape, or act

**Dorsal Shutdown (freeze/collapse)** feels like:

- Numbness or disconnection
- Foggy thinking, difficulty concentrating
- Heavy limbs, lack of energy
- Feeling spacey or not quite present

**Social Engagement (safe)** feels like:

- Relaxed muscles, easy breathing
- Interest and curiosity
- Ability to connect with others
- Sense of being present in your body

**My observations:**

**Day 1:** Time/situation: ______________________________________________

State I noticed: ______________________________________________

Body sensations: ______________________________________________

**Day 2:** Time/situation: ______________________________________________

State I noticed: ______________________________________________

Body sensations: ______________________________________________

**Day 3:** Time/situation: ______________________________________________

State I noticed: ______________________________________________

Body sensations: ______________________________________________

**Patterns I'm beginning to notice:**

_______________________________________________________________________________

_______________________________________________________________________________

_______________________________________________________________________________

_______________________________________________________________________________

**Notes:** Mark the first moment each day you notice a green-zone cue.

_______________________________________________________________________________

## What to Expect From This Workbook

Let's talk about what healing actually looks like, because it probably won't match the picture you have in your mind.

You might imagine healing as a steady upward line: each week better than the last, symptoms gradually fading, until one day you wake up and realize you're "fixed." Real healing looks more like a spiral. You'll revisit the same issues at different depths. You'll have breakthroughs followed by what feel like setbacks. You'll make progress, then find yourself back in familiar patterns, wondering if anything has actually changed.

This is how your body learns.

Your nervous system won't release years of protection all at once. That would be overwhelming and potentially retraumatizing. Instead, healing happens in layers. You'll work with one pattern of tension, and as it releases, something underneath might surface. You'll expand your capacity to feel a little more, to stay present a little longer. Then your system might need to retreat, to consolidate what it learned before going further.

This workbook is designed to honor that nonlinear process. Each chapter builds on the previous one, but you don't have to move through them in strict order. If a particular exercise feels too intense, skip it and come back later. If you find yourself drawn to a section that speaks to what you're experiencing right now, start there. Your body knows its own pace better than any book can prescribe.

The structure follows a logical progression: understanding what Complex PTSD does to your body, learning to recognize your nervous system states, developing tools to regulate those states, working with specific body patterns where trauma is held, and gradually building capacity for more aliveness and presence. But your actual healing path might zigzag through these territories, spending more time in some areas than others, returning to foundational practices when you need them.

You might worry: "What if I can't feel anything?" This is common, especially if you've lived primarily in shutdown or disconnection. Numbness is a form of protection, and it won't release until your nervous system feels safe enough. The practices in this book will help you develop sensation awareness gradually. You'll start where you are, with whatever you can feel: maybe just the pressure of your feet on the floor or the temperature of your hands. Sensation will return in its own time.

Or you might worry the opposite: "What if I feel too much?" If your system tends toward hyperarousal, you might be afraid that paying attention to your body will make the anxiety worse. The concept of "window of tolerance" will be your guide. This is the zone where you can feel sensation and emotion without becoming overwhelmed. All the practices in this book are designed to help you stay within or gradually expand this window, never pushing you into overwhelm.

When you do bump up against your edges (when an exercise brings up more than you can handle), that's important information. You'll learn to recognize when you're approaching the boundary of your window and how to back off, to titrate the experience, to work with smaller doses.

Some key principles will guide your work:

**Titration** means taking things in small, manageable amounts. Work in sips: ten seconds with a sensation, ten seconds with an anchor. Instead of diving into the most overwhelming trauma memory, you'll work with small sensations, brief moments of awareness, gentle practices that don't flood your system. You might spend weeks just learning to take a full breath or noticing tension in your shoulders. This is the pace at which your nervous system can actually integrate change.

**Pendulation** means moving between sensation and ease, between activation and rest. Touch the tight spot, then look at something that feels kind, then return. You won't stay in difficult territory continuously. You'll touch into something challenging, then consciously shift your attention to something neutral or pleasant, allowing your system to oscillate rather than getting stuck. This back-and-forth teaches your nervous system that you can approach difficulty and return to safety.

**Resourcing** means identifying what genuinely helps you feel steadier. Name three reliable supports you can access within one minute. This might be different from what you think should help. A resource could be a memory of a place you loved, a pet's warmth, the feeling of your favorite sweater, or simply the weight of your body in a chair. You'll build a repertoire of resources you can turn to when things feel overwhelming, anchors that remind your nervous system it's not alone in that old trauma anymore.

The goal is a steadier relationship with your nervous system: to understand its language, to work with it rather than against it, to develop the capacity to move between states with more ease. You're learning to recognize these states when they happen, to have tools for navigating them, and to spend increasing amounts of time in states where you feel present, connected, and alive.

Your nervous system is always taking in new information, always adapting, even when you can't see the changes. Trust that your body wants to heal. It's been trying all along. You're just learning to work with it more skillfully.

Be gentle with yourself. You're doing something brave: turning toward sensations and experiences you've spent years avoiding or numbing. That takes courage. When you feel frustrated with your pace, remember you're rewiring patterns that have been in place for years or decades. Give yourself the same patience you'd give a child learning to walk. There will be stumbling. That's part of learning.

On slow days, return to one anchor: the weight of your feet or the warmth in your hands.

---

## ✎ EXERCISE: Setting Your Healing Intentions

---

Rather than creating goals to achieve, this exercise invites you to identify qualities you want to cultivate in your healing journey.

Complete the following:

*Three qualities I want to cultivate:*

1. ______________________________________________

2. ______________________________________________

3. ______________________________________________

*Examples might include: presence, self-compassion, curiosity, patience, safety, aliveness, connection, peace, groundedness, trust*

*What feeling more of this quality might look like in my daily life:*

______________________________________________

______________________________________________

______________________________________________

*One small way I can practice this quality this week:*

______________________________________________

______________________________________________

*My commitment to myself as I begin this work:*

______________________________________________

______________________________________________

______________________________________________

*Notes: Copy your top quality onto a sticky note where you'll see it.*

# Chapter 2:
# Meeting Your Nervous System

*"The greatest source of our suffering is the lies we tell ourselves about our own experience." — Gabor Maté*

You're at a family gathering, surrounded by people you love. Someone raises their voice in laughter. Your heart starts racing. Your chest tightens. You want to run. Your rational mind knows you're safe, but your body has already made a different decision.

This happens more often than you'd like to admit. A raised voice, a certain tone, even just the feeling of too many people in one room, and suddenly you're back in that familiar state of alarm. You tell yourself you're overreacting. You try to talk yourself down. Nothing works. Your body has already left the conversation.

This disconnect between knowing you're safe and feeling safe is one of the most frustrating aspects of Complex Post-Traumatic Stress Disorder (Complex PTSD). You can understand logically that the danger has passed. You can recognize that the present moment is different from the past. But your nervous system operates on a different timeline, making decisions about threat and safety before your conscious mind even gets a vote.

Here's what most people don't tell you: this isn't a failure of willpower or a sign that you're broken beyond repair. Your nervous system is doing exactly what it was trained to do. It learned its lessons early and learned them well. The problem isn't the system itself but what it learned to protect you from.

This chapter is about learning to speak your body's language. Not to override it or convince it that it's wrong, but to understand what it's trying to tell you. Once you can recognize the patterns, you can begin to work with your nervous system instead of fighting against it. You can start teaching it new information, one small signal of safety at a time.

## The Three States That Run Your Life

Your nervous system operates in three distinct states, each with its own physiology, its own emotional tone, and its own way of seeing the world. You move between these states dozens of times a day, often without noticing. But when trauma is involved, you can get stuck in states that were meant to be temporary, living in emergency mode when there's no emergency, or shutting down when you need to be present.

### Safe and Social: Ventral Vagal

The first state is what researchers call ventral vagal, but you can think of it simply as your safe and social state. This is where connection happens. Your voice has natural variation and warmth. You can make eye contact without effort. Laughter comes easily. Your body feels relaxed but alert, your breathing is smooth and effortless, and the world seems manageable. You can think clearly, respond flexibly, and access your sense of humor. This is the state where you feel like yourself.

**Mobilized: Sympathetic Activation**

When threat appears, or when your nervous system perceives threat, you shift into sympathetic activation. This is mobilization. Your heart rate increases, your muscles tense, blood flow redirects to your limbs. You're ready to fight or run. At its best, this state gives you energy and focus. You can meet a deadline, stand up for yourself, or handle an urgent situation. But when trauma has sensitized your system, sympathetic activation can feel like constant anxiety. Your jaw clenches. Your shoulders creep up toward your ears. You feel irritable, defensive, ready to argue or escape. Sleep becomes difficult because your body refuses to believe the danger has passed.

**Shutdown: Dorsal Vagal**

If sympathetic activation doesn't resolve the threat, or if the threat feels too overwhelming to fight or flee from, your nervous system has one more option: dorsal vagal shutdown. This is immobilization. Everything slows down. You feel heavy, disconnected, like you're watching your life through thick glass. Your thinking becomes foggy. Time feels strange, either moving too fast or not at all. This is the state of freeze, collapse, and dissociation. It's your nervous system's last-ditch effort to protect you from unbearable overwhelm. If I can't escape the danger, your body reasons, I'll escape from myself.

Here's what matters: none of these states are inherently bad. You need all three. Ventral vagal for connection and daily life. Sympathetic for motivation and meeting challenges. Dorsal vagal for deep rest and recovery. The problem isn't having these states but getting stuck in them, or moving between them so rapidly that you never feel stable.

Complex PTSD often means living outside that safe and social state more than you live in it. You might spend most of your time in sympathetic hypervigilance, scanning for danger, unable to relax. Or you might collapse into dorsal shutdown, watching your life happen from a distance. Sometimes you toggle between them, feeling wired and exhausted at the same time, anxious and numb in the same moment.

In the previous chapter, you explored these states separately. Here you'll learn how your system moves between them—the sequence it follows like rungs on a ladder. From shutdown, you move up into activation, and from activation, you can reach safety. But the ladder also goes down. When sympathetic responses don't work, when fighting or running doesn't resolve the threat, you slide into shutdown. Understanding this movement helps you recognize where you are and what your system needs to shift.

Each state has its own worldview. In ventral vagal safety, problems seem solvable. Other people seem trustworthy. The future seems possible. In sympathetic activation, everything looks like a threat or a challenge. You're ready to defend, to push back, to prove yourself. In dorsal shutdown, nothing seems to matter. Connection feels impossible. Hope disappears. The world feels flat and distant.

Trauma doesn't just change which state you're in. It changes how you experience each state. Healthy sympathetic activation feels like energy and motivation. Trauma-triggered sympathetic activation feels like panic, rage, or the certainty that something terrible is about to happen. Healthy dorsal vagal feels like deep rest. Trauma-triggered dorsal feels like depression, hopelessness, and complete disconnection.

You might recognize yourself in one state more than others. Maybe you're always on edge, always preparing for the next crisis. Maybe you feel numb more often than you feel anything else. Maybe you can access moments of safety, but they're fragile, easily disrupted by the smallest trigger. All of this is information. All of this tells you something about what your nervous system learned and what it still expects.

---

### EXERCISE: Three States Body Map

---

This exercise helps you identify where you physically feel each nervous system state. Understanding these body sensations gives you early warning signs of state shifts.

Get three pieces of paper or use the space below. Draw a simple outline of a human body on each one (stick figure is fine).

**Instructions:**

1. Label the first drawing "Safe and Social (Ventral Vagal)"
2. Label the second drawing "Mobilized (Sympathetic)"
3. Label the third drawing "Shutdown (Dorsal Vagal)"

For each drawing, mark on the body where you typically feel that state. Use colors, words, symbols, or shading.

**Safe and Social might include:**

- Warm chest
- Relaxed shoulders
- Soft belly
- Grounded feet
- Open throat

*Where do you feel safety in your body?*

---------------------------------------------------------------------------

---------------------------------------------------------------------------

**Mobilized might include:**

- Racing heart
- Tight jaw
- Clenched fists
- Tense shoulders
- Shallow breathing high in chest
- Hot face

*Where do you feel activation in your body?*

_______________________________________________________________________________

_______________________________________________________________________________

**Shutdown might include:**

- Heavy limbs
- Foggy head
- Numb extremities
- Hollow chest
- Empty feeling
- Disconnection from body

*Where do you feel shutdown in your body?*

_______________________________________________________________________________

_______________________________________________________________________________

**After completing all three drawings, reflect:**

*Which state do you spend most of your time in?* ____________________________________________

*Which state is hardest to access?* _________________________________________________________

Keep these drawings as a reference. They'll help you recognize state shifts as they happen.

## Recognizing When You're Stuck in Fight, Flight, or Freeze

Learning to recognize your survival responses in real time is different from understanding them conceptually. These responses don't announce themselves clearly. You don't wake up thinking, "I'm in sympathetic activation today." Instead, you snap at your partner over something trivial. You can't sit still. You scrub the kitchen counters for the third time this week even though they're already clean.

The fight response feels like energy with nowhere to go. Your muscles stay tense, ready for confrontation. Your jaw aches from clenching. You notice yourself arguing more, even about things that don't matter. Someone offers help and you feel irritated rather than grateful. You want to push back, to prove something, to make others understand or back off. Your thinking becomes black and white. You're right or they're wrong. Safe or dangerous. With me or against me. The subtlety disappears. Everything becomes a battle, even when there's no real conflict.

Sometimes fight doesn't look aggressive. It can show up as rigid control. You micromanage every detail of your day. You make lists upon lists. You try to predict and prevent every possible problem. You can't delegate because no one else will do it right. This is still fight, just turned inward. You're trying to control your environment so tightly that nothing unexpected can threaten you.

Flight feels like restlessness that won't quit. Your thoughts race from one worry to the next. You can't finish tasks because you're already thinking about what comes next. Sitting still feels impossible. You stay busy, always busy, because stopping means feeling what you've been running from. You might physically leave situations, making excuses to escape conversations, events, or relationships. Or you might stay physically present while your mind checks out, planning your exit, counting the minutes until you can leave.

Flight can also look like chronic busyness. You fill every moment of your day. You say yes to too many commitments. You take on extra projects at work. You volunteer for things you don't have time for. You check your phone constantly. You scroll through social media for hours. Anything to keep moving, to keep your mind occupied, to avoid the stillness where uncomfortable feelings might catch up with you.

Freeze is the hardest to recognize because it often masquers as something else. You might look fine on the outside. You go to work, you have conversations, you complete basic tasks. But inside, you're gone. You stare at your phone for two hours without processing anything you're seeing. You sit down to do something and then can't remember what you sat down to do. Time disappears in strange ways. Suddenly it's evening and you don't remember the afternoon. You feel like you're moving through water, everything slow and effortful and distant.

Sometimes freeze shows up as an inability to make decisions. Every choice feels overwhelming, even simple ones. What to eat for dinner. Which shirt to wear. Whether to respond to a text message. Your mind goes blank when asked a question. You know you have thoughts and feelings about things, but you can't access them in the moment. You end up just going along with whatever others decide because forming your own preference requires more energy than you have.

Your body gives you different signals in freeze than in fight or flight. Fight and flight both involve activation, increased heart rate, muscle tension, mobilization. Freeze involves collapse. Your energy drops. Your limbs feel heavy. Your voice gets quieter, flatter. Eye contact becomes difficult. You might feel cold when others are comfortable. Your breathing becomes shallow but not rapid. You're not speeding up; you're slowing down. Shutting down. Disappearing from the inside while maintaining a shell of functionality.

Many people experience mixed states, especially with long-term trauma. You might feel simultaneously wired and exhausted. Anxious but numb. Ready to run but too heavy to move. This is sympathetic activation layered on top of dorsal collapse. Your body is trying to mobilize, but the shutdown response keeps pulling you under. You end up stuck between states, unable to fully access either, feeling awful in a way that's hard to describe to others.

You might also toggle rapidly between states. One moment you're angry and confrontational. The next moment you've collapsed into shutdown. Or you're anxious and restless, then suddenly you can't get off the couch. Your partner or friends might describe you as unpredictable or moody. But you're not trying to be difficult. Your nervous system is cycling through its options, trying to find something that works, never quite landing anywhere stable.

---

### EXERCISE: My Survival Response Pattern

---

This reflection helps you identify which survival responses you default to and in what situations.

**Read each statement and check all that apply to you:**

**FIGHT responses:**

☐ I often feel irritable or angry without a clear reason

☐ My jaw or fists stay clenched

☐ I argue or push back even over small things

☐ I need to be right or in control

☐ I feel defensive when people offer help

☐ I have urges to throw, break, or hit things

☐ I snap at people I care about

☐ I feel like I need to prove myself constantly

**FLIGHT responses:**

☐ My thoughts race and I can't slow them down

☐ I stay constantly busy to avoid feelings

☐ I have trouble sitting still or relaxing

☐ I make excuses to leave social situations

☐ I check my phone or scroll obsessively

☐ I take on too many commitments

☐ I feel restless, like I need to escape

☐ I avoid situations that might be uncomfortable

**FREEZE responses:**

☐ I lose track of time regularly

☐ I space out or dissociate during stress

☐ I feel numb or disconnected from my body

☐ I can't make decisions, even simple ones

☐ I stare at screens without processing information

☐ My mind goes blank when asked questions

☐ I feel heavy, like moving through water

☐ I appear functional but feel gone inside

**Now reflect:**

My primary survival response (the one I checked most) is: ________________________________________

This response shows up most often when: ________________________________________

A specific recent example: ________________________________________

My secondary response (second most checked) is: ________________________________________

I notice myself switching between responses when: ________________________________________

The survival response I use least is: ________________________________________

One thing I notice about my patterns: ________________________________________

There's no right or wrong pattern. This is simply information about how your nervous system learned to protect you.

## How Complex PTSD Hijacks Your Body's Safety Signals

Your nervous system learns early. Before you have language, before you have memories you can recall, your body is already taking notes. It's learning what safe feels like and what danger feels like. It's learning whether the world is trustworthy or threatening, whether people are sources of comfort or sources of harm.

When you grow up with consistent safety, your nervous system develops accurate threat detection. It can distinguish between real danger and false alarms. It knows when to activate and when to relax. It trusts that if something goes wrong, help will come. This is normal development, though fewer people experience it than we'd like to believe.

When you grow up with chronic trauma, particularly relational trauma from the people who were supposed to protect you, your nervous system learns different lessons. It learns that danger is constant. It learns that people are unpredictable at best, harmful at worst. It learns that safety is an illusion, a temporary state that could shatter at any moment. These lessons get encoded deeply, in places words can't reach.

This is the fundamental difference between single-incident trauma and Complex PTSD. If you experience one traumatic event as an adult, your nervous system has years of safety to fall back on. It knows the trauma was an aberration. It can eventually recalibrate. But if trauma is what you grew up with, if unpredictability and fear were your normal, your nervous system has no baseline of safety to return to. It never learned what true calm feels like. The alarm state became your default setting.

Your nervous system uses a process called neuroception to detect safety and danger. This happens unconsciously, below awareness, scanning your environment hundreds of times a day. Neuroception reads facial expressions, tones of voice, body language, environmental cues. It makes split-second decisions about whether you're safe or threatened. When it works properly, you feel at ease with safe people and alert around genuine danger.

Trauma breaks this system. Your neuroception becomes oversensitive, detecting threats that aren't there, missing safety signals even when they're present. A neutral facial expression looks angry. A slight change in someone's tone signals rejection. Silence feels threatening. Kindness feels suspicious. Your nervous system is working perfectly according to its programming, but the programming is based on a world that no longer exists.

This is why you can logically know you're safe while your body insists you're in danger. Your conscious mind has updated its information. Your nervous system hasn't. It's still operating on data from years ago, still preparing for dangers that belonged to your past, still trying to protect a child who needed protection that never came.

You might feel unsafe in situations that should feel good. Someone compliments you and your stomach drops. A partner is affectionate and you feel trapped. A friend wants to get closer and you want to run. Your nervous system has learned that good moments precede bad ones, that letting your guard down leads to pain, that trust is dangerous. So it keeps you vigilant even during positive experiences, maybe especially during positive experiences.

Time doesn't exist the same way in your nervous system as it does in your mind. Your prefrontal cortex knows it's 2025 and you're an adult with agency and choices. Your amygdala and brainstem are still back in the kitchen where your father raged, in the bedroom where you learned to disappear, in the car where no one spoke about what everyone knew was happening. When something in the present reminds your nervous system of the past, even slightly, the distance between then and now collapses. You're not remembering the trauma. Your body believes the trauma is happening right now.

This is why triggers can seem irrational. The threat your nervous system is responding to isn't in the present moment. It's in the pattern, in the resemblance, in some subtle cue that matched your history. A smell. A phrase. The way someone moved. The quality of light at a certain time of day. Your conscious mind doesn't even register the connection, but your body does. And your body responds accordingly.

Hypervigilance becomes your constant companion. You scan every room you enter, noting exits, assessing people, calculating threats. You monitor the moods of everyone around you, trying to predict their reactions, trying to stay one step ahead of potential danger. You can't relax in public spaces. You struggle to sleep because your guard stays up even in your own home. This isn't paranoia. This is your nervous system doing the job it learned to do, staying alert because relaxation once meant vulnerability.

The exhaustion this creates is real and physical. Your nervous system was designed to activate temporarily, then return to rest. But you live in activation, day after day, year after year. Your body never fully powers down. Your stress hormones stay elevated. Your muscles never completely release. You wake up tired because sleep doesn't restore you the way it should. You're not lazy or weak. You're running a marathon that never ends.

---

## ✏ EXERCISE: Safety Signal Confusion Log

---

This exercise builds awareness of when your nervous system signals danger despite objective safety. Understanding these moments is the first step toward teaching your body new information.

Think of three recent situations where you felt unsafe even though you were objectively safe. For each situation, record the following:

**Situation 1:**

What was happening?

________________________________________________________________________

________________________________________________________________________

What did your body feel? (heart rate, breathing, muscle tension, etc.)

___________________________________________________________________________

___________________________________________________________________________

What thoughts came up?

___________________________________________________________________________

What from your past might this have reminded your nervous system of?

___________________________________________________________________________

___________________________________________________________________________

**Situation 2:**

What was happening?

___________________________________________________________________________

What did your body feel?

___________________________________________________________________________

What thoughts came up?

___________________________________________________________________________

What from your past might this have reminded your nervous system of?

___________________________________________________________________________

___________________________________________________________________________

**Situation 3:**

What was happening?

___________________________________________________________________________

What did your body feel?

___________________________________________________________________________

What thoughts came up?

___________________________________________________________________________

What from your past might this have reminded your nervous system of?

___________________________________________________________________________

___________________________________________________________________________

**Reflection:**

What patterns do you notice across these situations?

---------------------------------------------------------------------------------------------------

What safety signals did your nervous system miss in these moments?

---------------------------------------------------------------------------------------------------

You're not trying to fix anything yet. You're simply building awareness of how your system operates.

## Why Your Body Reacts Before Your Mind Can Think

You've probably experienced this: someone says something, and before you can process their words, your chest is already tight. Your partner reaches toward you, and before you register it's a loving gesture, you've already flinched. You walk into a crowded room, and before you consciously decide how you feel about it, your body is already heading toward the exit.

This isn't a flaw in your processing. This is how your nervous system was designed. The parts of your brain responsible for survival, the amygdala and brainstem, operate much faster than your prefrontal cortex, the part that handles conscious thought and decision-making. The survival brain can detect and respond to a threat in about 200 milliseconds. By the time your thinking brain comes online to assess the situation, your body has already taken action.

This speed difference exists for good reason. In genuinely dangerous situations, thinking takes too long. If you had to consciously evaluate every potential threat, analyzing whether the movement in your peripheral vision was a stick or a snake, you'd be too slow to survive. Your survival brain makes quick, imperfect decisions that favor caution. Your nervous system follows the same rule: it would rather trigger too often than miss a real threat. One undetected danger costs more than a hundred false alarms.

The problem with trauma is that it calibrates this system incorrectly. Your survival brain learned to detect danger everywhere. It learned that caution isn't just useful but essential. It learned that the cost of missing a threat is devastating. So it prioritized sensitivity over accuracy. It would rather activate a hundred times unnecessarily than miss the one time activation could have saved you.

This means your body responds before you can think, and by the time your conscious mind catches up, you're already activated. Your heart is racing, your muscles are tense, your breath is shallow. You might try to think your way back to calm. You tell yourself there's no danger. You remind yourself this is different from the past. You try to be rational. None of it works. You can't think your way out of a body response because thinking wasn't involved in creating the response.

The signal starts in your body and only later reaches your awareness. First, your nervous system detects something, a cue of danger or safety that you're not consciously aware of. Then your body responds with changes in heart rate, breathing, muscle tension, hormones. Then you feel the emotional result of these physical changes: fear, anger, numbness. Finally, your thinking brain creates a story to explain what you're feeling. But the story comes last. By the time you're thinking about why you feel anxious, your body has been anxious for several seconds already.

This is bottom-up processing. The signal starts at the bottom, in the primitive survival centers of your brain and the sensory information from your body, and moves up to your conscious awareness. Most therapeutic approaches try to work top-down, using thinking and reasoning to change feelings and behaviors. But you can't override a bottom-up process with top-down strategies. Telling yourself to calm down when your body is screaming danger just creates more conflict. Your conscious mind says one thing, your survival brain says another, and your survival brain always wins because it controls your physiology.

Understanding this releases you from a lot of self-blame. You haven't failed when you "overreact." Your body did exactly what it was trained to do. You're not weak for being unable to think your way into calmness. That was never how the system worked. You're not too sensitive or too difficult or broken. You're responding precisely the way anyone would respond if they had learned the same lessons about danger and safety that you learned.

When someone tells you to "just calm down" or "think positive," they're asking you to use your prefrontal cortex to override your amygdala. But your amygdala isn't listening to your prefrontal cortex right now. It's busy keeping you alive, at least according to its outdated information. The real work isn't convincing your thinking brain that you're safe. Your thinking brain already knows. The real work is giving your body new experiences of safety, repeatedly and consistently, until your nervous system starts to update its threat detection.

This also means you need to change your relationship with your body's reactions. Instead of seeing them as problems to be solved or weaknesses to be overcome, you can start seeing them as information. Your body is telling you something. It might not be accurate information about the present moment, but it's always accurate information about what your nervous system learned in the past. When your heart races during a kind interaction, your body isn't wrong or broken. It's showing you that kindness once preceded harm, or that closeness once led to pain. That's valuable information. It tells you what needs healing.

---

### EXERCISE: Body Before Thought Tracking

---

For the next 24 hours, simply notice moments when your body reacted before your mind could think. You're not trying to change anything, just building awareness of this bottom-up process.

Throughout the day, catch 3-5 moments when your body responded before your thinking mind caught up. For each moment, briefly note:

**Moment 1:**

What triggered the response? (a sound, a look, a situation)

____________________________________________________________

What did your body do first? (stomach drop, shoulders tense, breath catch, etc.)

____________________________________________________________

What thought came after the body response?

____________________________________________________________

**Moment 2:**

What triggered the response? ____________________________________

What did your body do first? ____________________________________

What thought came after the body response? ____________________________

**Moment 3:**

What triggered the response? ____________________________________

What did your body do first? ____________________________________

What thought came after the body response? ____________________________

**Moment 4 (if applicable):**

What triggered the response? ____________________________________

What did your body do first? ____________________________________

What thought came after the body response? ____________________________

**Moment 5 (if applicable):**

What triggered the response? ____________________________________

What did your body do first? ____________________________________

What thought came after the body response? ____________________________

**End of day reflection:**

How many seconds typically passed between body reaction and conscious awareness?

-----------------------------------------------------------------------------------

What surprised you about this tracking?

-----------------------------------------------------------------------------------

This simple observation helps you understand that your body's responses aren't failures of willpower but automatic processes that happen before conscious choice.

## Mapping Your Personal Nervous System Patterns

Your nervous system has its own unique signature. The way you move between states, the triggers that push you out of safety, the warning signs that appear before you fully shift, these patterns are yours alone. They developed from your specific history, your particular experiences, the exact conditions you learned to navigate.

Two people with Complex PTSD might have completely different nervous system profiles. One might live in hypervigilance, always activated, always scanning. The other might spend most of their time in shutdown, dissociated and disconnected. One might have a narrow window of tolerance, easily pushed into dysregulation. The other might have learned to function through extreme states, maintaining performance while internally collapsed. There's no single way that trauma shows up in the nervous system.

Your early attachment relationships shaped your nervous system more than almost anything else. If your caregivers were consistently available and attuned, your nervous system learned that distress leads to comfort, that needs get met, that other people are sources of regulation. If your caregivers were inconsistent, unpredictable, or harmful, your nervous system learned different lessons. Maybe it learned that showing distress makes things worse, so it stopped signaling needs. Maybe it learned that connection itself is dangerous, so it avoids closeness. Maybe it learned to stay constantly vigilant because safety was temporary and fragile.

These early patterns still influence how you regulate now. If you learned to suppress your needs, you might struggle to ask for help even when you desperately need it. If you learned that connection is dangerous, you might push people away precisely when you're most dysregulated. If you learned that expressing feelings led to punishment, you might shut down emotionally even in relationships where expression would be welcomed. Your adult relationships replay these early templates until you consciously work to change them.

Your nervous system biography includes more than just attachment. It includes the specific ways danger showed up in your life. Was the threat loud or quiet? Explosive or insidious? Did danger arrive suddenly or build slowly? Was there physical violence, emotional abuse, neglect, or some combination? Each type of threat teaches the nervous system to look for specific cues. If danger was loud, your nervous system might be sensitive to raised voices. If danger was silent, it might respond to emotional withdrawal or subtle shifts in mood. Your particular history created your particular sensitivities.

You also developed personal strategies for managing threat. Maybe you learned to make yourself small and quiet. Maybe you learned to become helpful, anticipating others' needs before they expressed them. Maybe you learned to scan constantly, staying one step ahead of potential danger. Maybe you learned to disappear inside yourself when things got bad. These strategies worked once. They kept you safe in an unsafe situation. They're not serving you the same way now, but your nervous system doesn't know that yet. It's still using the tools that worked when you were young and powerless.

Understanding your patterns means becoming curious about your own experience without judgment. When do you tend to shift out of regulation? What specific situations, people, or environments push you toward activation or shutdown? What are your earliest warning signs that you're moving out of your window of tolerance? And just as importantly, what helps you shift back toward regulation? What environments, activities, or people support your nervous system in feeling safer?

Your window of tolerance is the range of activation where you can function well. Inside this window, you can think clearly, respond flexibly, connect with others, handle challenges. Outside this window, you're either in hyperactivation, anxious and overwhelmed, or hypoactivation, shut down and disconnected. Trauma typically narrows this window. Things that wouldn't bother someone with a wider window push you quickly into dysregulation. Part of healing is slowly widening this window, increasing your capacity to stay present through a broader range of experiences.

You might notice your window is narrower in certain contexts. Maybe you can handle stress at work but fall apart in intimate relationships. Maybe you're fine alone but dysregulate in groups. Maybe mornings are okay but evenings push you toward shutdown. These variations are important information. They tell you where your nervous system feels most threatened and where it has access to more resources.

Creating a personal nervous system map isn't about diagnosis or pathology. You've been adapting to what you lived through, not failing to heal. This map is a practical tool, a reference guide to your own patterns. It helps you predict when regulation might be difficult. It helps you recognize early warning signs before you're fully dysregulated. It helps you identify what supports your system needs. Most importantly, it helps you develop compassion for your own experience. Your nervous system is doing its best with the information it has.

---

### EXERCISE: My Nervous System Map

---

This comprehensive reflection creates your personal nervous system profile. Take your time with this. Return to it over several days if needed. This becomes a reference document you'll use throughout the workbook.

**PART 1: MY COMMON TRIGGERS**

List situations, people, environments, or experiences that tend to push you out of regulation:

1. ____________________________________________________________________

2. ____________________________________________________________________

3. ____________________________________________________________________

4. ____________________________________________________________________

5. ____________________________________________________________________

What do these triggers have in common?

______________________________________________________________________

**PART 2: MY DEFAULT SURVIVAL RESPONSES**

When I'm stressed or triggered, I tend to:

☐ Fight (get angry, defensive, argumentative)

☐ Flight (want to escape, stay busy, avoid)

☐ Freeze (shut down, go numb, disconnect)

☐ Mixed states (describe): ________________________________________

My earliest warning signs of dysregulation (before I'm fully activated or shut down):

Physical: ______________________________________________________________

Emotional: _____________________________________________________________

Behavioral: ____________________________________________________________

Thoughts: ______________________________________________________________

**PART 3: MY NERVOUS SYSTEM HISTORY**

How did I learn to respond to threat in childhood?

______________________________________________________________________

______________________________________________________________________

What worked to keep me safe then?

______________________________________________________________________

______________________________________________________________________

What strategies am I still using that might not serve me now?

---

---

## PART 4: WHAT HELPS ME FEEL SAFER

Environments that support my regulation:

---

Activities that help me shift toward safety:

---

People who help me feel grounded:

---

Things that make dysregulation worse:

---

## PART 5: MY WINDOW OF TOLERANCE

On a scale of 1-10, how wide is my window of tolerance? (1 = very narrow, 10 = very wide)

Current rating: _______

My window is narrower when:

---

My window is wider when:

---

## PART 6: PERSONAL NOTES

What I most want to remember about my nervous system:

---

---

---

One thing I learned about myself from this mapping:

---

---

Keep this map accessible. Update it as you learn more about your patterns. This is your nervous system's user manual, written by the person who knows it best: you.

# Chapter 3: Learning to Feel Safe in Your Own Skin

*"Safety is not the absence of threat; it is the presence of connection."*
*— Stephen Porges*

You're sitting in your living room on a quiet Sunday afternoon. Nothing is wrong. No one is angry. No crisis is unfolding. The light coming through the window is soft. Your favorite tea is cooling in the mug beside you. And yet your shoulders are up near your ears. Your jaw is clenched. Your stomach is tight. You scan the room, listening for sounds, waiting for something to go wrong.

This should be relaxing. You know that. But relaxation feels like leaving your post. Like dropping your guard right before the attack comes. Your body learned a long time ago that peace is temporary, that calm is the setup, that letting your shoulders drop means you won't see the next blow coming.

Here's what most people don't understand about trauma: the hardest part isn't facing the pain. It's learning to tolerate feeling safe. Your nervous system, after years of operating in survival mode, has come to interpret safety as a threat. Stillness feels dangerous. Good moments trigger bracing. The absence of chaos feels like the calm before the storm.

You're not broken for feeling this way. Your body is doing exactly what it was trained to do. It kept you alive by staying vigilant, by never fully resting, by treating every moment of peace as potentially deceptive. The problem is that this strategy, which once protected you, now prevents you from healing.

Healing requires safety. Not just the intellectual understanding that you're safe, but the felt sense in your body that you can let down, even slightly, even for a moment. This is where the real work begins. Not in excavating trauma, not in analyzing your past, but in rebuilding your nervous system's capacity to recognize and tolerate the present moment when it's actually okay.

This chapter isn't about convincing you that you're safe. It's about teaching your body, gradually and gently, that it's possible to feel safe. We start small. We start with seconds, not hours. We start with noticing, not forcing. We build the capacity for safety one micro-moment at a time, because that's the only way it can be built.

## Why Feeling Safe Is the Foundation of Healing

Your therapist tells you to talk about the trauma. Your friend suggests you just need to process it. The self-help book promises that confronting your past will set you free. But here's what they're missing: your nervous system can't process anything when it's in survival mode.

Dr. Stephen Porges's polyvagal theory gives us the roadmap. Your autonomic nervous system has three main states: ventral vagal (safe and social), sympathetic (fight or flight), and dorsal vagal (freeze and shutdown). Healing happens in the ventral vagal state. That's when your prefrontal cortex comes online, when you can think and feel simultaneously, when you can integrate experiences instead of just surviving them.

When you're in fight-or-flight or freeze, your brain literally cannot do the work of healing. It's like trying to have a rational conversation while someone is chasing you with a knife. Your body is focused on survival, not integration. This is why trauma therapy without establishing safety first can retraumatize. You're asking your nervous system to process threatening material while it's already perceiving threat everywhere.

But here's where it gets complicated: you might be objectively safe and still not feel safe. You might be in a comfortable home, with supportive people, with no actual danger present, and your body is still screaming that something is wrong. This is the gap between being safe and feeling safe, and it's the gap that trauma creates.

Your nervous system learned to associate certain cues with danger. A tone of voice. A time of day. The sound of footsteps. A particular kind of silence. These cues trigger your threat response even when no actual threat exists. Your body is responding to the past as if it's happening now. You can repeat that you're safe a hundred times, but your body will only believe it when experience—not thought—proves it true.

There's another layer here that makes this even more complex: for many trauma survivors, safety feels dangerous. Your body associates letting your guard down with being hurt. Relaxation was when the bad thing happened. Trust was when you got betrayed. Vulnerability was when you got attacked. So your nervous system, trying to protect you, keeps you in a state of hypervigilance. It's convinced that if you relax, even for a moment, something terrible will happen.

This is why "just relax" is such useless advice. Your body isn't being difficult. It's being protective. It's running an old program that once kept you alive. The work isn't to override this protection, but to slowly, gently update the program by giving your nervous system new information.

We also need to talk about co-regulation versus self-regulation. You learned what safety feels like through someone else's calm presence—your caregiver's heartbeat, voice, and steadiness. That shared regulation installed your first sense of safety. Your nervous system learned to regulate by borrowing calm from someone else's nervous system.

If you didn't get consistent co-regulation as a child, or if your attachment figures were themselves dysregulated or dangerous, you didn't get to install that felt sense of safety. You're not starting from a deficit in self-regulation skills. You're starting without ever having learned what regulation feels like in the first place.

This means two things: first, beating yourself up for struggling to self-regulate is missing the point entirely. You're trying to do something you were never taught. Second, healing often requires co-regulation before self-regulation. Being around calm, regulated people. Working with a therapist whose nervous system can help settle yours. Letting your dog's steady breathing help slow your heart rate. You're not weak for needing this. You're working with how nervous systems actually function.

The path forward isn't about forcing yourself to feel safe. It's about creating conditions where your body can begin to recognize safety when it's actually present. We're teaching your nervous system a new language, and like any language, it's learned through repeated, gentle exposure, not through one dramatic insight.

We start with seconds. A moment when you notice your breath slow. A split second when your shoulders drop slightly. A brief instant when you're not scanning for danger. These micro-moments are the seeds. We're not trying to feel safe all the time. We're building the capacity to tolerate feeling safe some of the time, in small doses, without immediately bracing for the next threat.

---

**EXERCISE: Noticing Micro-Moments of Safety**

---

For the next 24 hours, notice when your body relaxes even slightly. You're not trying to create safety, just catching when it naturally occurs.

What happened and what you noticed in your body:

______________________________________________________________________________

______________________________________________________________________________

______________________________________________________________________________

______________________________________________________________________________

______________________________________________________________________________

Any patterns?

______________________________________________________________________________

## Creating Your First Anchor of Safety

Deb Dana, a clinician who specializes in polyvagal theory, introduced the concept of "glimmers." These are the opposite of triggers. Where triggers are cues that activate your threat response, glimmers are tiny moments when your nervous system registers safety, even briefly. They're subtle. A stranger smiling at you on the street. The way light filters through leaves. Your friend's laugh. The warmth of your coffee mug in your hands.

Most trauma survivors have been trained to scan for danger. Your attention is pulled toward what could go wrong, what might hurt you, what you need to defend against. This makes sense. But it also means you miss the glimmers. Your nervous system needs data that says "this is okay." Glimmers provide that data, but only if you notice them.

The practice here is simple but requires intention: you're training your attention to catch these moments. Not to create them or force them, but to notice when they naturally occur. Each time you notice a glimmer, you're sending your nervous system a message: "See? This moment is safe. We can register this."

Let's get practical. Your nervous system is regulated through your senses. This isn't metaphorical or psychological. It's physiological. What you see, hear, touch, smell, and taste directly impacts your autonomic state. This means you can use sensory input to help shift your nervous system toward safety.

The key is finding what actually works for your nervous system, not what you think should work or what works for other people. Your friend might find lavender calming. You might find it cloying. Someone else might love weighted blankets. You might feel trapped. There's no universal answer. You need to discover your own sensory anchors through experimentation.

Touch can be grounding. Some people find soft textures soothing. Others prefer something with more resistance. A smooth stone you can roll in your palm. A piece of velvet. Your own skin, brushing your thumb across your fingers. The cool surface of a wall. The texture of your dog's fur. You're looking for touch that helps your body settle, even marginally.

Sound matters more than most people realize. Not background noise, but specific sounds that your nervous system recognizes as safe. For some, it's music without words. For others, it's nature sounds: rain, ocean waves, wind in trees. Some people find comfort in low, steady tones. Others need rhythmic patterns. White noise. A fan. Someone's voice. The sound of your own humming.

Scent goes directly to your limbic system, the emotional center of your brain. This is why smell can be so powerful for regulation. What scent makes you feel more settled? Coffee? Pine? The smell of rain on pavement? Your partner's shirt? Mint? Vanilla? You're not looking for pleasant. You're looking for regulating.

Taste can also be an anchor. The sharpness of ginger. The sweetness of honey. The cold of ice water. The bitterness of dark chocolate. Sour candy. Peppermint. Something crunchy that requires attention to chew. You're using taste to bring yourself into your body and the present moment.

What you see affects your nervous system state. Natural light versus artificial light. Looking at the horizon versus being in a small space. The color of your walls. Looking at something alive (a plant, a pet). Photos of places or people that feel safe. The sky. Trees. Water. Even the angle of your gaze matters. Looking up slightly can increase activation. Looking down or soft-focusing can support calming.

Now we add another layer: orienting. This is a practice from Somatic Experiencing, developed by Peter Levine. Orienting means using your eyes and body to take in your actual present environment and notice that you're safe right now. Not thinking about whether you're safe, but letting your body register it through sensory input.

Here's how it works: you slowly turn your head and let your eyes scan your environment. Not frantically, not anxiously, but with curiosity. You're looking for what's actually here. The lamp in the corner. The tree outside the window. The edge of the table. Your dog sleeping on the floor. You're letting your nervous system gather information: "I am here. This is my environment. Right now, in this moment, there is no threat."

This practice interrupts the trauma response, which pulls you into the past or into imagined future threats. Orienting brings you back to what's real and present. Your body can't be in full threat response while simultaneously taking in benign environmental details. The two states are incompatible.

You're building a menu of resources. Not a rigid plan, but a collection of options you can reach for when you need them. Some days, one thing will work. Other days, you'll need something different. The goal is having choices, knowing you have access to sensory experiences that help your nervous system shift toward safety, even slightly.

One more thing: the difference between distraction and regulation. Distraction pulls your attention away from what you're feeling. Regulation helps your nervous system shift states. Scrolling your phone might be distraction. Feeling the weight of a stone in your hand might be regulation. Watching TV might be distraction. Listening to a specific piece of music while noticing how your body responds might be regulation.

Distraction isn't bad. Sometimes you need it. But it doesn't build capacity. Regulation does. Regulation teaches your body that it can move from activation back to calm, that it has agency, that it can influence its own state. This is the skill you're building.

---

### EXERCISE: Five Senses Safety Inventory

---

Find one thing for each sense that helps you feel even slightly calmer. Actually try each one and notice your body's response.

TOUCH: ______________________________________________

SOUND: ______________________________________________

SCENT: ______________________________________________

TASTE: ______________________________________________

SIGHT: ______________________________________________

## Grounding Techniques That Actually Work

You've probably been told to ground yourself. Maybe a therapist suggested it. Maybe you read it in an article. The advice usually goes: "When you feel anxious, use the 5-4-3-2-1 technique. Name five things you can see, four things you can touch, three things you can hear, two things you can smell, one thing you can taste."

So you try it. You're in the middle of a panic attack, heart racing, can't breathe, and you're supposed to count objects in the room. You try. You name things. Sometimes it helps a little. Often it doesn't help at all. Sometimes it makes things worse because now you're panicking AND feeling like you're failing at the one thing that's supposed to help.

Here's what's often missing from grounding advice: not all grounding techniques work for all people, and some standard techniques can actually increase activation for trauma survivors. The 5-4-3-2-1 method works by engaging your thinking brain, but when you're in high activation, your thinking brain is offline. You're asking your brain to do something it literally cannot do in that state.

Trauma-informed grounding works differently. It doesn't try to think your way out of activation. It gives your body direct physical information that you're in the present moment, supported by the earth, in contact with solid things that hold you.

Let's start with the most basic grounding tool you have: gravity. Right now, wherever you're sitting or standing, you're being held by the surface beneath you. The chair is supporting your weight. The floor is beneath your feet. Gravity is pulling you down into this support. Your body knows this, but your attention might not be there.

Bring your attention to where your body makes contact with solid surfaces. If you're sitting, notice your sit bones pressing into the chair. Feel the chair pushing back, supporting you. Notice the backs of your thighs, your back against the backrest. If your feet are on the floor, feel them there. Not just thinking about it, but actually sensing the pressure, the contact, the support.

This is grounding: bringing your awareness to your body's physical connection with something solid. You're giving your nervous system information through sensation, not through thought. "I am here. I am held. I am supported by something solid."

Your feet are particularly powerful for grounding because they have so many nerve endings and because standing or walking requires you to be in your body. If you're able to stand, try this: press your feet firmly into the floor. Not stomping, not aggressive, just steady pressure. Notice the floor pressing back. Rock slightly forward and back, feeling how the weight shifts. This gives your body clear sensory information about where you are in space.

If standing isn't available or doesn't feel safe, you can create similar grounding through your hands. Press your palms flat against your thighs, against a wall, against a table. Feel the solid surface. Press and release, press and release. You're using pressure and contact to remind your body where its edges are, where you end and the world begins.

Some people find hand-on-heart helpful. One hand on your heart, one on your belly. Not forcing anything, just contact. The warmth of your own hands on your body. Some people find this soothing. Others find it activating or uncomfortable. Try it. Notice what happens. If it doesn't help, don't force it.

Temperature can be grounding. Cold water on your wrists. Holding ice in your hand. Splashing cold water on your face. Cold activates your dive reflex, which can shift your nervous system out of panic. Warm water can also ground. Washing your hands slowly, noticing the temperature, the sensation. A warm shower. Heat from a heating pad. You're looking for temperature that brings your attention into your body and the present moment.

Bilateral stimulation is another tool. This means alternating stimulation on both sides of your body. It's used in EMDR therapy, but you can use simple versions on your own. Butterfly taps: cross your arms over your chest and tap your shoulders alternately, left, right, left, right, at a pace that feels calming. Or tap your thighs. Or march in place. The alternating pattern can help settle your nervous system.

Humming or making sound can be grounding because it requires breath and creates vibration in your body. The vibration of your own voice can be calming. Low tones tend to be more regulating than high tones. You don't need to hum loudly or for long. Even 30 seconds of low humming can shift your state.

Here's what doesn't work: forcing yourself to ground aggressively. If you're gripping your hands into fists, clenching your jaw, demanding your body calm down NOW, you're actually increasing your threat response. Your body interprets that aggression as danger. Grounding needs to be gentle, an invitation, not a command.

You're also not trying to make anxiety disappear instantly. You're offering your nervous system information. "I am here, in this body, in this moment, with these feet on this floor." Sometimes that's enough to create a slight shift. Sometimes it isn't. That's okay. You're practicing, not performing.

If a grounding technique isn't working, don't fight with it. Try something else. Sometimes you need movement. Sometimes you need stillness. Sometimes you need to lie down with weight on top of you. Sometimes you need to go outside. Your body knows what it needs, but it takes practice to hear it.

One more thing: grounding isn't about forcing yourself to feel better. It's about helping your body recognize where and when you are. You're not in the past. You're not in the trauma. You're here, now, with feet on ground, breath in lungs, held by gravity.

---

### ✏ EXERCISE: Finding Your Grounding Stance

---

Try each method for 30-60 seconds. Rate how much it helped (0-10).

Pressing feet into floor: _____

Pressing palms against surface: _____

Cold water on wrists: _____

Hand on heart and belly: _____

Butterfly taps on shoulders: _____

Low humming: _____

**My top 3:**

1. ______________________________________________________________________________
2. ______________________________________________________________________________
3. ______________________________________________________________________________

## Building a Toolkit for When You Feel Overwhelmed

The time to build a lifeboat is before the storm, not during it. When you're in the middle of overwhelm, when your heart is racing and your thoughts are spiraling and you can barely breathe, that's not the moment to figure out what might help. Your thinking brain is offline. You need something prepared, something you can reach for without having to make decisions.

This is why we build the toolkit now, while you're relatively calm. You're gathering resources while you have access to your prefrontal cortex, so that when you don't, the path is already there.

First, let's clarify what we mean by overwhelm. Your nervous system has a threshold. Below that threshold, you can handle stress. You might not like it, but you can function. Above that threshold, you move into overwhelm. Your body shifts into survival mode: fight, flight, freeze, or fawn. Once you're there, your capacity to help yourself drops dramatically.

The goal is twofold: catch yourself before you cross that threshold when possible, and have tools ready for when you cross it anyway. Because you will. Everyone does. Overwhelm isn't failure. It's being human, especially if you're carrying trauma.

Let's build your toolkit in layers.

**Layer One: Quick Interventions (Under One Minute)**

These are things you can do immediately when you notice activation rising. You want three options minimum so that if one doesn't work, you have others.

Physical reset options: splash cold water on your face, hold ice, do five jumping jacks, step outside, press your back against a wall, stomp your feet, clap your hands. You're using physical input to interrupt the activation pattern.

Breath options: exhale longer than you inhale (breathe in for four counts, out for six), or sigh breath (breathe in through your nose, sigh out through your mouth with sound). You're not taking deep breaths, which can increase anxiety. You're extending your exhale, which activates your parasympathetic nervous system.

Sensory options: smell something strong (peppermint oil, coffee, lemon), listen to a specific song you've identified as calming, look at a photo that makes you feel safer, touch something with strong texture.

**Layer Two: Longer Regulation Practice (5-15 Minutes)**

When you have more time and need deeper regulation, you need one practice you can turn to. This might be a body scan, a specific breathing pattern, a grounding meditation, gentle movement, or a somatic practice like shaking or swaying.

The key is having one practice that you've done before, that you know helps, that you don't have to think about. You follow the familiar path because your body knows it.

**Layer Three: Connection Resource**

One person you can reach out to. Not someone who will fix it or need you to explain everything, but someone whose presence helps regulate your nervous system. This might be a friend you can text, a therapist, a crisis line, or even a voice message you record to yourself during a calm moment.

The goal isn't always to talk about what's happening. Sometimes it's just to hear a calm voice, to feel less alone, to borrow some regulation from someone else's nervous system.

**Layer Four: Physical Object**

One thing you can hold. A stone, a piece of fabric, a photo, a small object that fits in your pocket. Something tangible that connects you to safety or to a moment when you felt okay. You can carry this with you. When you need it, you hold it, feel its weight, its texture. It's a physical anchor.

**Layer Five: When Nothing Works**

This is the hard truth: sometimes nothing works right away. You try your tools and you're still overwhelmed. Your body is still activated. You still can't breathe right.

This is when you need permission to ride it out. You need a reminder that panic attacks end, that flashbacks end, that overwhelm peaks and then subsides. It's temporary, even though it doesn't feel that way.

Your reminder might be a note you write to yourself now: "This is temporary. This will pass. I am not in danger. My body is doing what it was trained to do. I don't need to fix this right now. I just need to survive the next five minutes."

Some people find it helpful to set a timer. Five minutes. You commit to just surviving for five minutes. When the timer goes off, you're usually through the worst of it. If not, you set it again.

You might need to get horizontal. Lie on the floor. Let the ground hold you. Remind yourself that you're allowed to fall apart. You don't have to be functional right now. You can just be here, breathing, waiting for the wave to pass.

Your toolkit isn't about never feeling overwhelmed. It's about having options, having prepared pathways, knowing you're not helpless even when you feel helpless. It's about practicing these tools when you're calm so they're available when you're not.

One more thing: use your tools before you hit overwhelm, not after. If you notice activation rising, use a tool. Don't wait until you're in full panic. The earlier you intervene, the more effective your tools will be. This is pacing. This is titration. This is working with your nervous system instead of fighting it.

---

**EXERCISE: My Regulation Toolkit Blueprint**

---

Three things under 1 minute when activated:

1. ____________________________________________
2. ____________________________________________
3. ____________________________________________

One longer practice (5-15 min): ______________________________

One person I can reach out to: ______________________________

One physical object that helps: ______________________________

One reminder when nothing works: ______________________________

## The Window of Tolerance and Why It Matters

As you saw earlier, this zone—called the window of tolerance—describes the range where you can stay present and connected. Inside this zone, you can think and feel at the same time. You can be stressed but still function. You can be sad but still cope. You can be triggered but still come back. Your emotions are present but manageable. Your thoughts are available. You can connect with others. You can make decisions. You can learn.

Above the window: hyperarousal. This is fight or flight. Your heart races. Your thoughts spin. You feel panicked, enraged, terrified, out of control. You can't think clearly. You might lash out or run away. Your body is flooded with activation, pumping out cortisol and adrenaline, preparing for battle or escape.

Below the window: hypoarousal. This is freeze or collapse. You feel numb, disconnected, exhausted, hopeless. You can't access your emotions. You might dissociate, zone out, feel like you're watching yourself from outside your body. Your energy plummets. You can't motivate. Everything feels heavy and impossible.

Both states are survival responses. Both are your nervous system trying to protect you. Neither is wrong or bad. But neither allows for healing, connection, or growth. You need to be inside your window for those things.

Here's what trauma does: it shrinks your window. What used to be a wide range of tolerable activation becomes narrow. Small stressors push you out of the window. A tone of voice sends you into hyperarousal. A moment of disappointment drops you into collapse. You spend more time outside your window than inside it.

This response isn't weakness—it's your body's way of staying prepared for a world it once found unsafe. Your nervous system learned that the world is dangerous, that threats are everywhere, that you need to be ready to fight or shut down at any moment. It's keeping the window narrow to protect you. The problem is that a narrow window makes life extremely difficult. You're either activated or shut down with very little space in between.

Healing means widening your window. Not overnight. Not through force. But gradually, through repeated experiences of moving toward the edge of the window and coming back to center. This is called pendulation, and it's how we build capacity.

You practice moving slightly into activation, then returning to regulation. You practice feeling slightly more emotion than feels comfortable, then grounding back into your body. You're teaching your nervous system that it can handle more range, that going near the edge doesn't mean you'll fall off, that you have tools to bring yourself back.

You can't force your window wider. You can only invite it, practice it, give your nervous system evidence that it's safe to have a wider range. Each time you approach the edge and come back, your nervous system learns. "Oh, we can go this far and still be okay. We can feel this much and still return to center."

This takes time. If you've spent years in a narrow window, you're not going to have a wide window next week. But you can widen it incrementally. A little more range this month than last month. A few more situations you can tolerate without tipping into overwhelm or shutdown. Progress is measured in millimeters, not miles.

You need to know your warning signs. What tells you you're approaching the top of your window? Racing thoughts? Clenched jaw? Tight chest? Irritability? Feeling like you want to run or fight? These are your cues. When you notice them, that's the moment to use your tools. That's when you practice bringing yourself back into the window before you fully exit it.

What tells you you're approaching the bottom of your window? Heaviness? Numbness? Disconnection? Feeling like nothing matters? Exhaustion that sleep doesn't fix? These cues mean you're moving toward collapse. You need different tools here than you do at the top. You might need movement to bring activation up. Music with a beat. Cold water. Anything that generates a little more energy.

Your window isn't static. It changes based on context, stress, sleep, physical health, time of day, who you're with. Your window might be wider in the morning than at night. Wider when you're rested than when you're depleted. Wider when you're with safe people than when you're alone.

This is normal. You're not failing when your window narrows. You're responding to conditions. The practice is noticing when your window is narrow and adjusting accordingly. Maybe you don't take on the difficult conversation today. Maybe you give yourself more grounding time. Maybe you lower your expectations and just focus on staying inside whatever window you have available.

The other piece is learning what typically pushes you out of your window. Certain people? Certain environments? Lack of sleep? Not eating? Anniversaries of traumatic events? Sensory overload? The more you understand your patterns, the more you can prepare. You can't always avoid triggers, but you can be ready with your tools when you know they're coming.

Some trauma survivors spend so much time in hyperarousal that they don't recognize it anymore. It feels normal. Their baseline is anxious, vigilant, on edge. They think everyone lives this way. If this is you, it means your window has shifted up. You're living above your optimal range without realizing it.

Others spend so much time in hypoarousal that numbness feels like home. They can't remember the last time they felt genuinely excited or connected. They move through life in a fog. If this is you, your window has shifted down. You're living below your optimal range.

Part of healing is finding center again. Not through force, but through gentle practice. If you're living above your window, you practice settling. If you're living below your window, you practice bringing in more activation. Both are working toward the same goal: finding the middle, expanding the range.

You might notice pendulation happening naturally once you start paying attention. You have a moment of anxiety, then you calm. You feel something painful, then you disconnect slightly, then you come back. Your nervous system is already doing this work. You're just learning to do it more consciously, more deliberately, with more skill.

The goal isn't to stay in your window all the time. That's not realistic. Life will push you out. Trauma reminders will push you out. Stress will push you out. The goal is spending more time inside your window than outside it, and developing the ability to return to your window when you leave it.

This is the difference between someone who's been traumatized and someone who's healing from trauma. Not that one never leaves their window, but that one can come back. You practice coming back. That's the skill. That's what we're building.

You also learn that leaving your window isn't catastrophic. You've left it before. You've survived. You've come back. The more you practice this, the less terrifying it becomes. You start to trust that even if you tip into panic or numbness, you have ways to return. You're not stuck there forever.

Some days your window will be wide. You'll handle stress well. You'll feel capable. Other days your window will be tiny. A small thing will send you spiraling. This doesn't mean you're regressing. It means you're human. Windows fluctuate. Healing isn't linear.

What you're building is the awareness to notice where you are relative to your window and the skills to work with that information. "I'm at the top of my window right now. I need to use my calming tools." Or "I'm below my window. I need to bring in some activation." Or "I'm in my window. I can handle this conversation."

You're also building compassion for yourself when you leave your window. You're not failing. Your nervous system is doing what it knows how to do. You're just learning to guide it back, to offer it resources, to widen the range gradually so that more of life becomes tolerable.

This is patient work. Your window didn't narrow overnight, and it won't widen overnight. But each time you notice where you are, each time you use a tool, each time you practice returning to regulation, you're building capacity. You're sending your nervous system the message that it can handle more range, that the world isn't as dangerous as it once was, that there's space to feel and think and stay present.

That's what healing looks like. Not perfect calm. Not never being triggered. But a wider window, more tools, more awareness, more ability to come back to yourself when life pushes you away.

---

### EXERCISE: Tracking My Window

---

What pushes me into hyperarousal (anxiety/panic):

_______________________________________________________________________________

_______________________________________________________________________________

Warning signs: _________________________________________________________________

What helps: ___________________________________________________________________

What pushes me into hypoarousal (numb/shutdown):

_______________________________________________________________________________

_______________________________________________________________________________

Warning signs: _________________________________________________________________

What helps: ___________________________________________________________________

When is my window wider? ______________________________________________________

When is it narrower? ___________________________________________________________

# Chapter 4: Befriending Your Body Again

*"The body is the shore on the ocean of being." — Sufi saying*

Sarah stands in front of her bathroom mirror, but she's not looking at her reflection. Her eyes focus somewhere past the glass, on a point in the middle distance. She's learned to get ready this way: brushing her teeth, washing her face, fixing her hair, all without actually seeing herself. It's a skill she perfected years ago, this ability to tend to her body while remaining utterly disconnected from it.

When she does accidentally catch her own gaze, there's a split second of vertigo. Who is that person? The face is familiar, but it belongs to someone else. Her body feels like a rental car she's been driving for years without reading the manual. Something functional but foreign, something she operates but doesn't inhabit.

If you recognize this experience, you're not alone. Many trauma survivors describe their relationship with their body in similar terms: enemy territory, a prison, a betrayer, a stranger. The body that was supposed to protect you became the site of violation, pain, or overwhelming sensation. It held terror you couldn't escape and sensations you couldn't control. Of course you left. Of course you learned to live from the neck up, treating everything below as something to be managed, ignored, or fought against.

The disconnect was brilliant survival. When feeling meant suffering, not feeling made perfect sense.

But here's the paradox healing asks of you: the very body you abandoned holds the key to your freedom. The sensations you learned to avoid contain the information your nervous system needs to finally complete its defensive responses, to discharge what's been trapped, to learn that the danger has passed. You can't reason your way out of trauma, because trauma isn't stored in thoughts. It lives in the clenched jaw, the tight shoulders, the held breath, the frozen pelvis.

This chapter isn't about forcing you to "love your body" or practice toxic positivity about physical sensations. It's not about yoga poses or green smoothies or looking at yourself in the mirror while reciting affirmations. Those approaches often miss the mark entirely for trauma survivors because they skip over the fundamental problem: your body doesn't feel safe to inhabit.

What follows is something different. This is about negotiating a truce. About building tentative trust, one small sensation at a time. About discovering that beneath the pain and disconnection, your body has been waiting. Not to hurt you again, but to help you heal.

The journey back home to your body is slow and careful. It requires infinite gentleness. And it starts with understanding why you left in the first place.

## Why You Might Fear Your Own Physical Sensations

You're sitting in a meeting when it happens. A flutter in your chest. Your first instinct isn't curiosity, it's panic. *Not here. Not now.* You hold your breath, trying to suppress the sensation before it grows into something bigger. You've learned from experience that noticing body sensations can open a door you won't be able to close. That flutter could become a racing heart, which could become a full panic attack, which could mean leaving the meeting, explaining yourself, feeling humiliated.

Better to just... not feel it.

This pattern even has a name: interoceptive avoidance, meaning the learned habit of turning away from bodily sensations that once signaled danger. If you have trauma, you're probably an expert at it. Interoception is your ability to sense internal bodily states: hunger, thirst, heart rate, muscle tension, gut feelings. For most people, interoception is helpful information. For trauma survivors, it often predicts danger.

Your body learned through repeated experience that certain sensations preceded terrible things. A knot in your stomach preceded your father's rage. Shakiness in your legs preceded being overwhelmed. Tightness in your chest preceded panic. Your nervous system, trying to protect you, drew a logical conclusion: if I can stop feeling these sensations, I can stop the terrible things from happening.

Except you can't actually stop the terrible things by suppressing the warning signals. All you can do is stop knowing they're coming.

So you learned to turn down the volume on your internal experience. You started living in your head, where thoughts are manageable and controllable. You might have used substances to numb sensation. You might have stayed constantly busy so you never had to be still enough to feel. You might have developed elaborate rituals to avoid situations that might trigger bodily sensations. You might have dissociated, your consciousness simply leaving your body during times of overwhelming sensation, like a circuit breaker flipping off to prevent damage.

The problem is this: you can't selectively numb. When you turn down the volume on pain, you also turn it down on pleasure, joy, connection, and aliveness. The same disconnection that protected you from feeling terror also prevents you from feeling love, excitement, or peace. You survived, but at the cost of truly living.

And there's another cost. The sensations you're avoiding don't disappear. They accumulate. They become the chronic tension in your shoulders, the digestive problems, the mysterious pain that doctors can't explain. They become the free-floating anxiety that seems to have no source. Your body is still trying to communicate with you, but you've stopped listening, so it has to speak louder.

Maybe you're afraid that if you start paying attention to your body, you'll discover something unbearable. That you'll uncover the full weight of what you've been carrying. That you'll be flooded with sensations or memories you can't handle. That you'll fall apart and won't be able to put yourself back together.

These fears make sense. Your past experience taught you that feeling leads to being overwhelmed. But here's what's actually true: the overwhelm comes from feeling too much, too fast, without the skills to regulate. What you're going to learn in this chapter is different. You're going to learn to approach sensation slowly, carefully, with tools to stay regulated. You're going to learn the difference between sensing and flooding.

The path forward isn't to feel everything all at once. It's to build capacity gradually, like strengthening a muscle that's been atrophied from disuse.

---

### EXERCISE: Naming the Fear

---

Before you can befriend your body, you need to acknowledge what makes it feel unsafe. Read each prompt and write whatever comes up. No censoring or judging.

When I think about tuning into my body, I'm afraid I'll feel:

__________________________________________________________________

__________________________________________________________________

The part of my body I'm most disconnected from is ____________________________ because:

__________________________________________________________________

__________________________________________________________________

If I started paying attention to my body sensations, I worry that:

__________________________________________________________________

__________________________________________________________________

What I need in order to feel safe exploring body sensations:

__________________________________________________________________

__________________________________________________________________

*After completing these prompts, notice if there are common themes. Simply naming these fears is the first step toward working with them.*

## The Difference Between Sensing and Reacting

Your heart is racing. Within seconds, your mind has already written the story: *I'm having a panic attack. Something's wrong. I need to get out of here.* You're halfway to the door before you realize you were just walking up a flight of stairs. The racing heart was simply your cardiovascular system doing its job, but your nervous system interpreted neutral information as danger.

This is the problem trauma creates: you lose the ability to distinguish between sensation and threat. Everything the body does becomes suspect. A tight throat means you're about to cry in public. A flutter in your chest means anxiety is coming. Tension in your shoulders means you're not safe.

But sensation itself is neutral information. Your body is constantly generating sensations: the contact of your feet on the floor, the movement of breath in your lungs, the temperature of your skin, the position of your spine. These sensations are just data. They tell you what's happening in your internal environment, nothing more.

The reaction (the meaning you assign, the emotion that follows, the behavior you engage in) comes from your nervous system's interpretation of that data. And when you have trauma, your nervous system is working with faulty information. It learned in the past that certain sensations predicted danger, so now it treats all similar sensations as threats, even when you're safe.

Here's what makes healing possible: you can learn to observe sensation without immediately reacting to it. You can create space between "I notice tightness in my chest" and "I am anxious." That space is where regulation lives.

Think of it this way. You have three types of awareness available to you:

Interoception is your awareness of internal bodily sensations: your heartbeat, your breathing, tension in your muscles, sensations in your gut. This is the information coming from inside your body.

Proprioception is your awareness of your body in space: where your limbs are, how you're positioned, whether you're balanced or off-kilter. This is the information about your body's relationship to physical space.

Exteroception is your awareness of the external environment: what you see, hear, smell, taste, touch. This is information coming from outside your body.

Trauma typically hijacks interoception. The internal landscape becomes so threatening that you either avoid it completely (dissociation, numbing) or become hypervigilant to it (constantly scanning for signs of danger). But you can learn to relate to interoceptive information differently, to notice it without being controlled by it.

The practice is simple but profound: become the witness. Instead of being the sensation, you observe the sensation. Instead of "I am anxious," you say "I notice anxiety in my body." Instead of "I'm falling apart," you say "I notice intense sensations in my chest and throat."

This isn't just semantic, it's neurological. When you can observe sensation, you're activating a different part of your brain than when you're consumed by sensation. You're engaging your prefrontal cortex, the part that can witness and reflect, rather than just your amygdala, the part that screams danger. This engagement allows your nervous system to stay regulated even in the presence of uncomfortable sensation.

The goal isn't to eliminate uncomfortable sensations. You'll always have them. You're a living human with a complex nervous system. The goal is to increase your capacity to be with sensation without immediately needing to change it, fix it, understand it, or make it go away.

This capacity is the foundation of everything else in this workbook. When you can notice sensation without flooding, you can track your nervous system states. When you can be with discomfort without dissociating, you can process trapped survival energy. When you can distinguish between sensation and story, you can reality-test your nervous system's threat assessments.

Start practicing the language shift. Every time you catch yourself saying "I am [emotion]," try rephrasing it as "I notice [sensation in body]." You might be surprised how much this simple change creates breathing room.

---

**EXERCISE: Sensation Without Story**

---

Set a timer for 3 minutes. Choose one body sensation to focus on: your feet on the floor, your back against the chair, your hands in your lap, or your breath moving.

For 3 minutes, describe only the physical sensations using these words: cool, warm, tingly, numb, heavy, light, tight, loose, pulsing, pressure, sharp, dull, smooth, rough, empty, full, still, moving.

*What I notice:*

____________________________________________________________

____________________________________________________________

____________________________________________________________

*If your mind creates stories or interpretations, simply notice that and return to pure sensation. Practice this daily for one week, each time with a different body area.*

## Starting Small When Everything Feels Too Much

You've tried meditation. The instructor said to "scan your body with gentle awareness," and within thirty seconds you were somewhere else entirely: thinking about your grocery list, planning tomorrow's meetings, anywhere but in your body. Or worse, you started scanning and got hit with such a wave of sensation or emotion that you had to stop, convinced this practice isn't for you.

Neither of these responses means you're broken or doing it wrong. They mean you're trying to take on too much too fast. Diving into full body awareness when you have trauma is like trying to run a marathon when you've been bedridden for months. You need to start smaller. Much smaller.

Titration means approaching the body in doses small enough to stay manageable. You're not trying to feel everything. You're practicing feeling one small thing successfully and then pausing. Each successful encounter with sensation builds your capacity for the next one.

Think about learning to swim. You don't start by jumping into the deep end. You start by putting your toes in the water. Then your ankles. Then maybe you sit on the steps. You gradually acclimate, building tolerance as you go. Body awareness works the same way.

The hands and feet are often the safest entry points. They're far from the vulnerable core of your body where trauma typically lives. They have lots of nerve endings, so they're easy to feel. And they're constantly in contact with something (the floor, your lap, the chair) which gives you concrete sensation to anchor to.

Start with what feels tolerable right now. If noticing your whole hand feels like too much, notice just your thumb. If that's too much, notice just the tip of your thumb. You're looking for the smallest possible unit of awareness that you can sustain without dissociating, numbing out, or getting flooded.

This is the edge: the place where you're feeling something but not overwhelmed by it. Too far from the edge and you're not building capacity; you're just staying in your comfort zone. Too far past the edge and you're flooding, which doesn't build capacity either. It just retraumatizes. The healing happens right at that edge, where there's a tiny bit of stretch but you're still in control.

Some of you reading this might be thinking, "But I feel nothing. I'm completely numb." If that's your experience, titration still applies. You start by simply placing your attention on a body part, even if you can't feel anything there yet. The noticing itself (the act of directing attention) begins to wake up neural pathways. Sensation might not come immediately, but the practice of checking in creates the possibility for sensation to return when your nervous system feels safe enough.

You have complete permission to go slowly. Healing is not a race. Going slowly is not a sign of weakness or failure; it's a sign of wisdom. Your nervous system will tell you how fast it can move. Listen to it.

---

### EXERCISE: One Fingertip of Awareness

---

Sit comfortably. Bring all your attention to just the tip of your index finger on your right hand for 30 seconds. Notice temperature, texture, tingling, pressure, or nothing at all.

After 30 seconds:

- Could you keep attention there? ☐ Yes ☐ Somewhat ☐ No
- Did you notice sensations? ☐ Yes ☐ Somewhat ☐ No
- Did you feel safe? ☐ Yes ☐ Somewhat ☐ No

If that felt okay, try two fingertips (index and thumb) for 30 seconds.

- Could you maintain attention? ☐ Yes ☐ Somewhat ☐ No

If that felt okay, try your whole right hand for 30 seconds.

- Could you maintain awareness? ☐ Yes ☐ Somewhat ☐ No

What this taught you:

-----------------------------------------------------------------------------------------

-----------------------------------------------------------------------------------------

*This is how small you can make the entry point. Anytime full body practices feel overwhelming, come back to one fingertip.*

## Gentle Body Scanning for Trauma Survivors

The standard body scan meditation asks you to lie down, close your eyes, and systematically move your attention through every part of your body from head to toe. For trauma survivors, this can be an exercise in overwhelm. Lying down is vulnerable. Closing your eyes removes visual orientation. Starting with the head means immediately encountering areas where trauma often lives: the jaw, the throat, the face. And the systematic, relentless progression doesn't allow for pausing, skipping, or backing out when you hit something too intense.

No wonder you might have tried body scanning once and decided it wasn't for you.

But body scanning (when modified for trauma) can be one of the most powerful tools for befriending your body. The key is doing it differently. You're extending an invitation, not issuing a command.

Here's how to make body scanning trauma-sensitive:

Start from the bottom. Feet and legs are typically less vulnerable than the core of your body. Beginning with your feet gives you a safer entry point and grounds you literally in contact with the earth. You can always return attention to your feet if things get intense elsewhere.

Move slowly. Take your time with each body area. This isn't a race to complete the scan. You're building relationship, and relationship requires patience. If you notice something interesting or difficult in one area, you can stay there, exploring gently, rather than pushing forward.

Use "flashlight awareness." Imagine moving a gentle beam of light through your body rather than harsh fluorescent overhead lighting that illuminates everything at once. The flashlight moves softly, revealing only what's in its immediate beam, leaving the rest in comfortable dimness.

Build in escape routes. Keep your eyes open if closing them feels too vulnerable. Sit up rather than lying down. Give yourself explicit permission to stop the scan at any point and return to your anchor (usually the breath or the sensation of your feet on the floor). You can skip body areas that feel too vulnerable. Your body, your pace, your choice.

Resource first. Before you begin scanning, establish a felt sense of safety. This might mean placing a hand on your heart, taking a few grounding breaths, or reminding yourself where you are and that you're safe right now. You scan from a place of relative stability, not from a place of already being activated. Notice the neutral and pleasant. Trauma trains you to scan for danger, to notice only what hurts or feels wrong. Intentionally include neutral and pleasant sensations in your awareness. The temperature of your feet. The softness of your clothing. The absence of pain in areas that feel okay. This retrains your nervous system to recognize that not everything in your body is a threat.

---

### ✎ EXERCISE: Safe Body Scan Practice

---

Sit comfortably with feet flat on the floor. Eyes open or softly lowered. Take three slow breaths. Remind yourself: *I am safe right now. I can stop at any time.*

**Feet and Ankles** (30 to 60 seconds) Notice contact with floor, temperature, weight, toes, ankles.

☐ Continuing ☐ Staying here ☐ Stopping

**Lower Legs** (30 to 60 seconds) Notice shins, calves, contact with chair, pressure, temperature.

☐ Continuing ☐ Slowing down ☐ Stopping

**Thighs and Pelvis** (30 to 60 seconds) Notice weight on chair, temperature. Option to skip pelvis.

☐ Staying ☐ Skipping to torso

Take three intentional breaths. ☐ Continuing ☐ Returning to feet ☐ Stopping

**Torso** (30 to 60 seconds) Notice back against chair, belly, breath movement. *If overwhelmed, return to feet immediately.*

Reality check: Name three things you see: ________________, ________________, ________________

**Shoulders and Neck** (30 to 60 seconds) Notice tension or ease, how neck holds head.

☐ Still okay ☐ Need break ☐ Done for today

**Arms and Hands** (30 to 60 seconds) Notice temperature, tingling, contact with surfaces.

**Face and Jaw** (optional, 30 to 60 seconds) *Only if feeling stable.* Notice jaw (clenched or loose?), forehead, eyes. *Return to feet if activated.*

After the scan: Take three breaths. Move your body. Wiggle, stretch, roll shoulders.

Which areas felt safe? ____________________________________________________________

Which did you skip? ____________________________________________________________

What did you learn? ____________________________________________________________

*Practice regularly. Some days you'll only scan feet and legs. That's perfect.*

## Turning Toward Sensation Without Getting Flooded

You're practicing noticing sensation in your body when suddenly everything intensifies. Your heart pounds. Your breathing gets shallow and fast. Your vision narrows. Thoughts scatter. You've crossed from noticing into flooding. Your nervous system has moved from activation into overwhelm. All the skills you were just using have gone offline. This is the razor's edge of somatic healing: you need to turn toward sensation to heal, but if you turn toward too much too fast, you flood your system and reinforce the very patterns you're trying to change. Flooding isn't healing. It's retraumatization.

So how do you approach sensation without drowning in it? The answer is pendulation: the rhythm of moving toward discomfort, then away to safety, then back toward discomfort again. Like waves on a shore. You don't stay submerged; you touch the edge and retreat, touch and retreat, gradually building your capacity to tolerate more. Remember your window of tolerance: the range where you can think, feel, and respond with flexibility. You might be uncomfortable, but you're not overwhelmed. Outside the window, you're either flooded (hyperaroused, panicked, fight or flight) or shut down (hypoaroused, numb, frozen). Healing happens inside the window. Just at the edge of it, where there's stretch but not breaking.

Pendulation keeps you in that window. You identify a mildly uncomfortable sensation (maybe tension in your shoulders). You bring your attention to it for a few seconds, noticing the tightness, the quality of it. Then, before it builds into overwhelm, you shift your attention away to something neutral or pleasant: the feeling of your feet on the ground, the coolness of air on your face, the support of the chair behind you. You rest there, letting your nervous system settle. Then you return to the uncomfortable sensation for a few more seconds. This creates a rhythm: approach, retreat, approach, retreat. Each time you approach discomfort and return to safety, your nervous system learns resilience. The knowledge that it can meet intensity in small doses and find relief again. The key is recognizing flooding before you're fully flooded. Everyone's signs are different, but common indicators include: Your thoughts become chaotic or you can't think at all. Your breathing changes (becomes very shallow and fast, or you hold your breath entirely). Your vision narrows or things look far away. You feel disconnected from your body or from reality. Your muscles get extremely tense or you feel paralyzed. Emotions intensify rapidly beyond what feels manageable. When you notice these signs, don't push through. Don't tell yourself you should be able to handle more. Don't shame yourself for hitting your edge. Instead, immediately shift your attention away from the difficult sensation to something safer: your anchor point. This might be: Your breath, slowing and deepening it deliberately. Your feet on the ground, pressing down slightly to feel that contact. The sounds in the room around you, orienting to the present. Your hands on your body in a comforting place, feeling that touch. Naming what you see: "Brown chair. Blue wall. Window."

Stay with your anchor until you feel your nervous system settle back into your window of tolerance. This might take thirty seconds or five minutes. There's no rush. You can return to the difficult sensation later if you choose, or you might be done for now. Either is fine. The practice isn't about conquering sensation. It's about building relationship with it. Each time you approach sensation and successfully retreat before flooding, you've completed a successful cycle. That success matters more than how long you stayed with the sensation or how intense it was.

---

## ✏ EXERCISE: Pendulation Practice

---

Sit comfortably. Take three breaths. Place feet flat on floor. This is your anchor.

**Identify Your Anchor** Bring attention to your feet for 30 seconds. Notice pressure, temperature, contact with ground. Can you feel your feet clearly? ☐ Yes ☐ Somewhat ☐ No

**Find Mild Discomfort** Scan for a sensation that's mildly uncomfortable (3 to 4 out of 10). Examples: shoulder tension, jaw tightness, stomach knot, chest tension.

The sensation I'm working with:

Location: ____________________________________________

Quality (tight, hot, sharp, heavy): ______________________________

Intensity 1 to 10: ______________________________________

**Practice Pendulation** You'll alternate between discomfort (5 seconds) and feet (10 seconds).

Round 1: Notice uncomfortable sensation (5 sec) then Feet (10 sec) ☐ Stayed regulated ☐ Some activation ☐ Flooded

Round 2: Notice sensation (5 sec) then Feet (10 sec) ☐ Stayed regulated ☐ Manageable ☐ Too much

Round 3: Notice sensation (5 sec) then Feet (10 sec)

Round 4: Notice sensation (5 sec) then Feet (10 sec)

Round 5: Notice sensation (5 sec) then Feet (10 sec)

Take three breaths. Move your body. Stretch, shake, roll shoulders.

Did the sensation change?

☐ Yes ☐ No

If yes, how? ____________________________________________

What did you notice about the rhythm?

____________________________________________________

*This is the basic pattern of somatic healing: small doses of discomfort alternating with safety. Practice regularly. It's the foundation for deeper trauma work.*

# Chapter 5:
# Understanding Dissociation and Coming Back Home

*"The greatest distance in the world is the fourteen inches between the mind and the heart." — Anonymous*

You're driving home from work and suddenly realize you don't remember the last twenty minutes. The scenery changed, you made turns, you stopped at lights, but you weren't there for any of it. Or you're sitting in a meeting, and you can see yourself from above, watching your own body speak words that sound like they're coming from someone else's mouth. Maybe you're having a conversation and you hear your voice, but it feels distant, like it belongs to a stranger. You're here, but you're not here. A ghost in your own life.

If this sounds familiar, you're experiencing dissociation—a survival reflex that activates when presence feels unsafe. When you couldn't escape physically, you escaped psychologically. Your body stayed, but your awareness left. It was a brilliant adaptation that kept you safe when nothing else could.

The thing is, dissociation doesn't always know when the danger is over. That protective mechanism that saved you during trauma can become a reflex, activating in moments that don't require escape. Just as you learned to leave, you can learn to come back. This chapter is your roadmap home.

## What Dissociation Really Means and Why It Happens

Dissociation is a disconnect, a break between thoughts, memory, surroundings, actions, and your sense of self—far beyond ordinary spacing out or losing yourself in a book. These pieces that normally fit together seamlessly come apart, and you experience yourself and the world through a fog, a screen, a distance that shouldn't be there.

When fight or flight aren't options, when you're too small or too trapped or too overpowered to run or defend yourself, your nervous system has one more card to play: leave. Not physically, but psychologically. Think of shutdown as staying in a house with all the lights turned off, and dissociation as leaving the house entirely while something else operates it on autopilot.

As a child, when the source of harm was also the person you depended on for food and shelter and love, fighting back wasn't an option. Running away wasn't an option. So you developed the capacity to be there and not be there at the same time. You floated up to the ceiling and watched. You focused on a spot on the wall until everything else disappeared. You went somewhere else in your mind, a place where this wasn't happening, where you were safe. It worked. It saved you.

Dissociation exists on a spectrum. On the mild end, you might zone out during conversations, lose track of what someone just said, or find yourself staring into space without realizing how much time has passed. In the middle range, you might experience depersonalization (feeling detached from yourself, like you're watching yourself from outside your body) or derealization (the world around you feels unreal, foggy, dreamlike, or behind glass). On the severe end, you might lose chunks of time entirely, finding yourself somewhere with no memory of how you got there, or losing connection to parts of your own experience or identity.

Your brain remembers. Even now, when stress, intimacy, or conflict arise, your system reaches for the same solution: leaving. The door is still open, and you're still walking through it, even when there's nowhere you need to escape from.

---

### ✏ EXERCISE: Dissociation Recognition Checklist

---

Read through the following experiences and check any that feel familiar to you. There's no judgment here, just recognition.

☐ Feeling like you're watching yourself from outside your body, as if you're an observer of your own life

☐ Feeling like the world around you is foggy, distant, or behind glass

☐ Losing chunks of time (minutes, hours, or more) with no memory of what happened

☐ Feeling disconnected from your body, like your hands or limbs don't belong to you

☐ Feeling like you're in a dream, even when you're awake

☐ Looking in the mirror and not recognizing yourself, or feeling like you're looking at a stranger

☐ Feeling emotionally flat or numb when you "should" be feeling something

☐ Having conversations where you hear your voice but it doesn't feel like yours

☐ Driving or performing tasks with no memory of doing them

☐ Feeling like you're floating, drifting, or not quite solid

☐ Experiencing the world as muffled or distant, like you're underwater

☐ Feeling smaller or younger than you actually are

☐ Not remembering important events or details from your past

☐ Feeling like there's a wall or barrier between you and other people

☐ Sensing that your emotions are happening "over there" instead of inside you

Notes on what you noticed:

________________________________________________

________________________________________________

________________________________________________

________________________________________________

## Recognizing the Signs You've Left Your Body

Dissociation can be so automatic that you don't notice it happening. One moment you're present, the next you're gone, and you only realize it later when you can't remember what someone just said or you find yourself wondering how you got through the last hour. Learning to catch dissociation earlier, to notice the moment you start to leave, gives you the chance to intervene before you're completely gone.

Your body gives you clues: numbness in your limbs, a floating sensation, vision narrowing. Emotionally, there's often a flatness—a space where feeling should be. You're in a situation that would normally produce emotion, worry, joy, anger, but there's nothing. Mentally, fog and confusion replace clarity. Following a conversation becomes difficult, like you're hearing words but they won't form meaning. Time distorts. You lose your train of thought mid-sentence.

Pay attention to when this happens. Dissociation has patterns. For some people, it kicks in with overwhelm: too much input, too many demands, and the system checks out. For others, it's conflict or criticism, the nervous system defaulting to escape the moment tension appears. Intimacy can be a trigger, physical or emotional closeness activating old danger signals. Even positive experiences can do it: success, praise, joy, moments when good things happen and some part of you learned long ago that good things are dangerous, that feeling too happy means pain is coming next.

The sooner you notice, the more options you have. You can't come back if you don't know you've left.

---

### EXERCISE: My Dissociation Early Warning System

---

Answer these questions to map your personal dissociation patterns:

**Physical sensations I notice when I start to dissociate:**

________________________________________________

________________________________________________

**Situations that most commonly trigger dissociation for me:**

________________________________________________

________________________________________________

**Things I tend to miss, forget, or lose track of when dissociated:**

________________________________________________

________________________________________________

**Signs others might notice before I do** (glazed look, not responding, going quiet, etc.):

________________________________________________

________________________________________________

**One early warning sign I'll pay attention to this week:**

________________________________________________

## Orienting to the Present Moment When You're Spacey

When you catch yourself drifting, spacey, only partially here, orienting brings you back. Orienting means deliberately using your senses to anchor yourself in present reality. Dissociation pulls you inward and away; orienting pulls you outward and back. Start with your eyes. This matters more than you might think. When you dissociate, your gaze often goes soft, unfocused, or fixed on one point. Your visual field narrows. Breaking this pattern starts with moving your eyes. Look around the room slowly. Not scanning quickly, but really looking. Let your gaze land on one object, notice it, then move to another. Follow the line where the wall meets the ceiling. Track movement if something is moving. Let your eyes do what they're designed to do: explore your environment.

While you're looking, start naming what you see out loud if you can, silently if you're around others. "Brown wooden table. Blue coffee mug. Window with white curtains. Green plant in the corner." Simple, factual observations. You're building a bridge back to concrete reality. The act of naming engages a different part of your brain than the part that's dissociating. Bring in touch. Place your hands flat on a surface and notice what it feels like. Press your feet firmly into the floor. If you're sitting, feel the chair supporting your weight. Notice temperature: is it cool or warm? Texture: smooth, rough, soft? Don't just think about it, actually feel it. Run your hand along the arm of the chair, touch something nearby, press your palm against the wall.

Use contrast to break through numbness. Cold water on your hands or face creates sensation strong enough to pierce the fog. Hold an ice cube. Splash cold water on your wrists. Or go the other direction: wrap your hands around something warm. The shift in temperature signals to your nervous system that you're here, in a body, in contact with the physical world. Movement helps. When stillness takes over, your body freezes and your awareness leaves. Gentle movement can bring you back. Stand up and walk. Stretch your arms overhead. Roll your shoulders. Tap your fingers on your thighs. Rock slightly back and forth. The physical sensation of movement contradicts the disembodied floating feeling of dissociation.

You're not demanding presence, you're making it easier to come back.

## EXERCISE: 5-4-3-2-1 Orienting Practice

Use this version of the practice specifically when you feel detached or unreal. If you notice anxiety increasing instead of decreasing, return to physical pressure through your feet and lengthen your exhale.

**5 things you can SEE:** Look around slowly, moving your head if needed. Name them out loud or write them below:

1. ______________________________________________
2. ______________________________________________
3. ______________________________________________
4. ______________________________________________
5. ______________________________________________

**4 things you can TOUCH:** Actually touch them. Notice the texture, temperature, and physical sensation:

1. ______________________________________________
2. ______________________________________________
3. ______________________________________________
4. ______________________________________________

**3 things you can HEAR:** Listen actively, even for subtle sounds:

1. ______________________________________________
2. ______________________________________________
3. ______________________________________________

**2 things you can SMELL:** Find them if you need to, even subtle scents count:

1. ______________________________________________
2. ______________________________________________

**1 thing you can TASTE:** Even if it's just saliva, notice the taste in your mouth:

1. ______________________________________________

After completing this practice, rate how present you feel (1 = very dissociated, 10 = fully present):

Before: _____ After: _____

## Reconnecting With Your Senses One at a Time

If full sensory engagement feels overwhelming, you can rebuild connection more gradually. One sense at a time. This approach works whether you're dealing with numbness (sensations feel distant or absent) or flooding (sensations feel too intense and you shut down to cope).

For many trauma survivors, some senses feel less safe than others—touch because it was violated, smell because it triggers memories, taste because it carries control or shame. Start with the sense that feels most neutral and build from there.

For many people, that's hearing. Music doesn't judge you. Sounds don't demand anything. You can listen without making yourself vulnerable. Put on a song and really listen. Not as background noise, but as your focus. Notice each instrument separately. Follow the bass line. Track the vocals. Let your attention rest on sound.

Sight can work similarly. Choose an object in your environment and really look at it. A plant, a picture on the wall, your own hand. Notice colors you didn't see before. Look at where light hits it. Notice shadows and shapes. Let yourself see details you usually overlook. Your eyes need something to do when you're dissociated, and giving them a job helps.

When you're ready to explore the more vulnerable senses, go slowly. For touch, you control the input. You choose what to touch, when, and how. Different textures provide different levels of stimulation. Soft fabrics can feel soothing. Rough surfaces like tree bark or concrete provide stronger sensation. Temperature matters: cold is alerting, warmth is often calming. Experiment to find what brings you back without overwhelming you.

Taste can be a powerful anchor if you approach it intentionally. Strong flavors cut through dissociative numbness: something sour, something minty, something spicy (within your tolerance). Eat something slowly, paying attention to how the flavor changes as you chew. Notice texture and temperature. You're using food as a sensory experience to ground you in your body.

Smell works quickly because it's processed by the brain areas linked to memory and emotion, which makes it both powerful and sensitive. Safe scents, ones you choose, can become anchors. Essential oils, coffee, fresh air, a specific soap. When you find a scent that feels grounding, keep it accessible.

Some people need more sensation, not less. If you're numb, if everything feels muted and far away, amplify the input. Turn up the music. Use stronger flavors. Seek out textures that create more sensation. Your nervous system needs enough stimulation to register that something is happening, that you're here and alive and sensing.

Others need less. If you're easily flooded, if sensory input quickly becomes overwhelming and you shut down to cope, you need gentler reentry. Dim lights, quieter sounds, subtler textures. You're training your system to tolerate sensation again without immediately dissociating to escape it.

### EXERCISE: Single Sense Exploration

Choose one sense to focus on for five minutes. Set a timer if it helps you stay with the practice.

**If you choose HEARING:** Listen to a piece of music. Name the instruments you hear:

______________________________________________________________________________

Notice when the volume or tempo changes:

______________________________________________________________________________

**If you choose TOUCH:** Explore three different textures. Describe what each feels like:

1. ____________________________________________________________________________
2. ____________________________________________________________________________
3. ____________________________________________________________________________

**If you choose TASTE:** Eat something slowly. Describe how the flavor changes:

______________________________________________________________________________

______________________________________________________________________________

**If you choose SMELL:** Notice every scent in your current environment:

______________________________________________________________________________

______________________________________________________________________________

**If you choose SIGHT:** Pick one object and look at it closely. Describe details you usually don't notice:

______________________________________________________________________________

______________________________________________________________________________

Which sense felt most accessible to you today? ________________________________________

Which sense might you explore tomorrow? ____________________________________________

## Building Presence Without Forcing It

Here's the paradox: the harder you try to stay present, the more likely you are to dissociate. Demanding that you stay here, berating yourself for leaving, forcing yourself to feel when you can't, all of this creates the exact conditions that trigger dissociation in the first place. Threat. Pressure. Overwhelm. Your nervous system does what it knows how to do: it leaves.

Dissociation is a protective part that learned to keep you safe. When you approach it with curiosity instead of criticism, when you work with it instead of against it, things shift.

Think about what triggers your dissociation. Now think about what dissociation protected you from. Did it protect you from feeling pain that would have been too much? From anger that wasn't safe to express? From terror that had nowhere to go? That part of you that dissociates is trying to keep you safe from experiences it learned were dangerous.

The question becomes: what would make it safe enough to stay present more often?

Sometimes the answer is time. Your system needs to learn, slowly, that presence doesn't equal danger anymore. Sometimes the answer is titration, tiny doses of presence at a time. You don't have to be fully here all at once. One percent more present than you were yesterday is progress. Feeling your feet on the floor for ten seconds counts. Noticing one sensation and then going back to autopilot is better than not noticing at all.

Some days, dissociation wins. You try all the techniques and nothing works. You're just gone, spacey, floating, and that's okay. On those days, practice harm reduction. Make sure you're physically safe if your awareness is limited. Ask for help if you need it. Don't make important decisions while you're dissociated if you can avoid it. Be kind to the part of you that needed to leave.

Other days, you'll have windows of presence. Moments where you're here, aware, feeling, connected. Those moments are what you're building toward. Not constant, unwavering presence, that's not realistic for anyone, but more frequent windows. Longer windows. Windows you can open more easily when you want to.

Small, consistent practices matter more than occasional intense efforts. Thirty seconds of orienting every day builds more presence than an hour of grounding exercises once a month. Your nervous system learns through repetition, through safe experiences repeated over time. Every time you return, even for a few seconds, you're rewriting the story your body learned about safety. This is how presence becomes possible again.

---

### EXERCISE: Negotiating With Dissociation

---

Write your responses to these prompts. Let whatever comes up be honest, not what you think you "should" say.

The part of me that dissociates is trying to protect me from:

______________________________________________________________________________

______________________________________________________________________________

What I needed this protection from in the past was:

______________________________________________________________________________

______________________________________________________________________________

What I need now to feel safe enough to be more present is:

________________________________________________________________________________

________________________________________________________________________________

One small practice I can do daily to build presence (even for 30 seconds):

________________________________________________________________________________

________________________________________________________________________________

I will do this practice at this specific time each day:

________________________________________________________________________________

**Track your practice this week:**

Day 1: Did it ☐ Didn't do it ☐

Day 2: Did it ☐ Didn't do it ☐

Day 3: Did it ☐ Didn't do it ☐

Day 4: Did it ☐ Didn't do it ☐

Day 5: Did it ☐ Didn't do it ☐

Day 6: Did it ☐ Didn't do it ☐

Day 7: Did it ☐ Didn't do it ☐

What I noticed over the week:

________________________________________________________________________________

________________________________________________________________________________

________________________________________________________________________________

________________________________________________________________________________

# Chapter 6:
# Releasing Suppressed Emotions Trapped in Your Tissues

*"The emotion that can be felt is not the one that lasts."*
Clarissa Pinkola Estés

Here's what no one tells you about emotions: they don't evaporate when you push them down. They don't dissolve because you're "being strong" or "moving on." They go somewhere. Specifically, they go into your body.

That tightness in your jaw that won't release? That's probably anger you couldn't express. The knot in your stomach that doctors can't explain? Likely fear or shame that had nowhere to go. The chronic tension in your shoulders, the mysterious pain that migrates through your body, the exhaustion that sleep doesn't fix: these aren't signs that something is wrong with you. They're signs that your body has been doing exactly what it needed to do to keep you safe: storing the emotions you couldn't afford to feel when they were happening.

Your body became a storage unit for everything that was too dangerous, too overwhelming, or too inconvenient to feel in the moment. And it's been waiting, sometimes for years, sometimes for decades, for permission to finally let those feelings move through and out.

This isn't some vague metaphor. The connection between suppressed emotions and physical symptoms is documented in neuroscience, validated in trauma research, and lived in the bodies of millions of people who've been told their pain is "all in their head." These experiences live in your tissues, your nervous system, your muscle memory. And the beautiful, hopeful truth is this: what's been stored can be released.

This chapter is about giving your body that permission. About learning to locate the emotions that live in your physical form, the anger in your clenched fists, the grief in your tight throat, the terror in your held breath. About finally feeling what you couldn't feel then, so you can be free now.

Your body has been tracking everything. Now you can help it settle the account.

## How Unfelt Emotions Become Physical Symptoms

Let's start with what emotions actually are: physical events. Emotions as real, measurable physical events involving hormones, neurotransmitters, muscle tone, heart rate, breathing, and blood flow.

When you experience something emotionally activating, your body prepares for action. Anger floods you with adrenaline and cortisol, tensing your muscles for fight. Fear does the same for flight. Sadness slows you down for withdrawal and seeking comfort. These are adaptive responses, your body doing exactly what evolution designed it to do.

Here's where the problem starts: emotions are meant to move. The word "emotion" itself comes from the Latin *movere*, to move, to move through. An emotion has a natural lifecycle: it arises, peaks, expresses itself through your body (crying, shouting, trembling, laughing), and then completes and subsides. The entire cycle might take 90 seconds to a few minutes when allowed to run its course.

But what happens when you can't complete the cycle? What happens when it wasn't safe to cry, scream, or shake? What happens when showing your anger meant punishment, or expressing your fear meant being called weak, or revealing your sadness meant burdening people who couldn't handle their own emotions, let alone yours?

Your survival brain makes a brilliant calculation: *This emotion is dangerous right now. Suppress it.*

And suppress it you do. You tighten your jaw to keep from yelling. You hold your breath to keep from crying. You tense your shoulders to contain the shaking. You clench your stomach against the nausea of fear. You literally use muscular tension to push the emotion down and hold it in place.

This works beautifully in the short term. You get through the moment. You survive. But that emotion doesn't disappear. The energy that was mobilized stays mobilized. The muscle tension that was meant to be temporary becomes chronic. Your body remains in a partial state of activation, waiting to complete an action that never comes.

Over time, this incomplete emotional response becomes physical symptoms:

- **Chronic pain** often corresponds to chronic muscular tension, your body still bracing against threats that have passed. The tension itself becomes painful, but it's also a signal: "There's something here I'm still protecting against."
- **Digestive issues** like IBS, nausea, and stomach pain frequently relate to held fear and anxiety. Your gut literally contracts against perceived danger. When the danger never resolves, the contraction never fully releases.
- **Inflammatory and autoimmune conditions** can be influenced by prolonged emotional stress, though this is a complex area that always requires clinical evaluation.
- **Chronic fatigue** makes sense when you understand how much energy it takes to continuously suppress emotion. You're running a containment operation 24/7. No wonder you're exhausted.
- **Tension headaches and migraines** often originate from chronic jaw clenching and neck tension, physical manifestations of anger, stress, and words that couldn't be spoken.
- **Fibromyalgia and chronic pain syndromes** frequently have their roots in unprocessed trauma and the full-body tension of living in survival mode.

These conditions are real. The body can express emotional suffering through physical symptoms, and they deserve medical attention and care.

The brilliant physician and trauma expert Gabor Maté puts it this way: "The body says what words cannot." Your symptoms are your body's language. They're the message, pointing toward what needs attention.

**Somatic memory**, the body-based memory of trauma and suppressed emotion, operates on a different system than conscious memory. You might not consciously remember the fear you felt at age four, but your body remembers. It's stored in the tension patterns, the startle responses, the places you habitually contract. Your tissues hold the memory of everything your mind has tried to forget.

Here's the hopeful part: because emotions are physical, they can be released physically. Your body is attempting to protect you and manage what it couldn't process. Because your body has been holding these incomplete responses, your body can also complete them. The tension that's been chronic for years can soften. The pain that's been mysterious can finally make sense and begin to resolve. The emotions that went underground can finally surface, move through, and release.

Your body has been waiting for you to be ready. For you to be safe enough. For you to have the resources to finally feel what you couldn't feel before. That time might be now.

---

### ✏ EXERCISE: Symptom-Emotion Connection Map

---

Your body may be trying to tell you something. This exercise helps you listen with curiosity.

**Identify 2-3 chronic symptoms you experience:**

1. ______________________________
2. ______________________________
3. ______________________________

**Choose one symptom to explore:** ______________________________

This symptom started or got worse around: ______________________________

When it's at its worst, I'm usually feeling: ______________________________

If this symptom could talk, it might be saying: ______________________________

______________________________

**What patterns are you noticing?**

______________________________

______________________________

*Note: This is exploration, not medical diagnosis. Continue working with healthcare providers while also considering emotional factors.*

______________________________

The grief you're carrying isn't just about events that happened, it's also about what *didn't* happen. The childhood you deserved but didn't get. The safety you needed but couldn't find. The protection, the nurturing, the unconditional love that should have been yours by birthright. You're mourning losses often invisible to others yet deeply significant.

Sadness has its own geography in the body:

- **The throat** is where grief gets literally choked back. The "lump in your throat" is the physical sensation of suppressed crying. Many people experience chronic throat tension, frequent throat-clearing, or feeling like they can't fully swallow. The throat is the gateway between your inner world and your voice; when sadness can't be expressed, it creates a blockage right there.

- **The chest and heart area** is where grief often manifests as heaviness or aching, sometimes described as heartache or heartbreak. The weight of unshed tears and unspoken sorrow sits right over your heart.

- **The belly and diaphragm** hold tension because deep sobbing comes from the diaphragm, so suppressed grief can create tightness in the belly and solar plexus. You might notice shallow breathing or inability to take full, deep breaths.

- **The eyes** show chronic tension from holding back tears. Some people describe a burning or pressure behind their eyes.

- **Overall heaviness** isn't just located in one spot. Grief can feel like a full-body heaviness, like you're carrying extra weight through your day.

The practice of working with grief requires something different than working with anger. Anger needs movement and expression. Grief needs witness and permission. Grief needs someone, even if that someone is your own adult self, to acknowledge that what happened *mattered*, that what you lost was *real*, and that your sadness is *legitimate*.

Many trauma survivors have never had their losses witnessed. No one acknowledged how bad it was. No one said, "I'm so sorry that happened to you. You deserved so much better." Sometimes you have to become that witness for yourself.

Grief takes shape when it finds space to flow in small doses. You might fear that if you start crying, you'll never stop. When you give it permission to move in contained amounts, it begins to complete. You can feel it in pieces, in waves, in doses you can handle.

The relief that comes from finally crying tears that have been held for years is profound. Something softens. Something releases. Something that's been clenched finally opens. Your body has been waiting to discharge this grief. When you give it permission, it knows exactly what to do.

### EXERCISE: Grief Body Listening

Place one hand on your heart and one on your belly. Close your eyes if safe. Take three slow breaths.

Gently ask yourself: *"Where am I holding sadness I haven't cried yet?"*

**I notice sensations in:** (check what applies)

☐ Throat

☐ Chest

☐ Belly

☐ Eyes

☐ Shoulders

☐ Overall body

☐ Other: ____________________

The sadness I'm carrying is about: ____________________________________________________________

____________________________________________________________________________________

What I lost (or never had) was: ____________________________________________________________

____________________________________________________________________________________

Place both hands on your heart and say:

*"I see this grief. I acknowledge this loss. What happened mattered. I'm here now."*

How my body feels after this practice: ______________________________________________________

____________________________________________________________________________________

____________________________________________________________________________________

## The Trembling, Shaking, and Tears That Heal

Watch an animal after it escapes from danger. A deer that's just run from a predator will stand still and begin to shake, not from cold or fear, but from the body's natural process of discharging stress hormones and completing the survival response. The shaking lasts a few minutes, then stops. The animal literally shakes it off and returns to grazing, nervous system reset.

Humans have this same built-in mechanism. We're designed to tremble, shake, cry, and sigh to discharge traumatic activation and return our nervous system to equilibrium. But unlike animals, we've been socialized to suppress these natural responses.

When you start to shake with fear or emotion, what were you told? "Calm down. Pull yourself together. Don't fall apart." When you started to cry, what happened? "Stop crying or I'll give you something to cry about." Or maybe it was more subtle: uncomfortable looks, awkward silence, people leaving the room, the sense that your emotional expression was burdening others.

You learned to suppress the body's natural healing responses. You learned to stay in control, to hold it together, to not let yourself "fall apart." And in doing so, you trapped the trauma activation in your nervous system with nowhere to go.

This section is about giving your body permission to do what it's been trying to do all along: complete the stress response through physical discharge.

Trembling and shaking signal that your body is releasing what it's been holding. The tremor comes from your nervous system discharging excess activation, literally shaking out the stress hormones that have been stored. This is called neurogenic tremoring, the nervous system's organic release mechanism.

David Berceli developed Tension and Trauma Releasing Exercises (TRE) based on this principle. The exercises activate the body's natural tremor mechanism, allowing it to release patterns of deep muscular tension created by difficult experiences. The trembling is involuntary but safe, your body doing exactly what evolution designed it to do. Crying is another powerful discharge mechanism. Emotional tears (as opposed to tears from cutting onions) actually contain stress hormones. Your body is literally excreting cortisol and other stress chemicals through your tears. Crying also activates your parasympathetic nervous system, the rest-and-digest response that calms you. This is why you often feel calmer, softer, and even sleepy after a good cry. Your nervous system has shifted states. That spontaneous deep breath or yawn signals your system rebalancing. Deep sighing and yawning are also discharge mechanisms, your body releasing tension and bringing your system back into balance.

The key to working with these natural releases is to approach them with titration, small doses, not overwhelming floods. Aim for contained, integrable releases within your window of tolerance. Here's the difference. Cathartic release means overwhelming, flooding, retraumatizing. You're swept away by the emotion, lose your sense of present safety, and end up more activated than before. Therapeutic release means contained, witnessed (by yourself or others), within your window of tolerance. You stay connected to present safety while allowing the emotion or tremor to move through.

The practice is to notice these natural discharge mechanisms when they start to happen and *allow* them instead of suppressing them. When you feel tears coming, let them come. When you feel a tremor in your legs or a shake in your hands, let it happen. When you feel the urge to sigh deeply, sigh. It's common to fear you won't be able to stop. In practice, the body tends to stop spontaneously when the discharge completes. Your body has its own wisdom. When the discharge is complete, when enough has moved through, it will naturally stop. The tremor will subside. The tears will dry. Your body knows how to regulate itself when you give it permission.

Some guidelines for safe release:

- **Start small:** You don't have to process everything at once. One minute of trembling or crying is valuable.
- **Stay present:** Keep some awareness of your current safety even while allowing the release.

- **Resource before and after:** Use grounding techniques before you start and soothing practices afterward.
- **Know when to stop:** If it starts to feel overwhelming, you can always pause. Place your hands on the ground, open your eyes, look around the room, remind yourself where you are.
- **Seek support when needed:** Some releases are best facilitated by a trained somatic therapist or TRE provider.

Your body has been holding trauma not because it's broken, but because it's brilliant. It stored what you couldn't process. Now, with safety and permission, it can finally let go.

---

**EXERCISE: Gentle Tremor Practice**

---

This is a 2-minute introduction to your body's natural tremoring. Keep it brief and contained.

Stand with feet hip-width apart. Very gently bounce your knees, tiny movements. Let your knees stay slightly bent. Continue the gentle bouncing for up to 2 minutes.

Notice if any trembling begins naturally. Don't force it. Just observe. If emotion arises, notice that too.

Stop. Stand still. Take three deep breaths.

Did any trembling occur? ☐ Yes ☐ No

If yes, where? ____________________________________________________________

Did emotions arise? ________________________________________________________

Did your body feel more or less tense after? _____________________________________

*Note: For deeper tremor work, consider working with a certified TRE provider.*

## Completing the Emotional Cycles Your Body Couldn't Finish

Let's bring all of this together: emotions are physical processes with a natural beginning, middle, and end. When allowed to complete, they move through your body, deliver their message, and resolve. But trauma interrupts this natural cycle.

An emotion that can't complete gets stuck mid-cycle. The activation remains in your system, waiting for resolution that never comes. You end up chronically activated, chronically tense, chronically braced, because your body is still trying to finish something that started years ago.

Here's what a complete emotional cycle looks like:

• **Activation:** Something happens and your body responds with an emotion, anger, fear, sadness, joy.

• **Peak:** The emotion reaches its maximum intensity. This is where the physical expression wants to happen, crying, shouting, trembling, laughing.

- **Expression and discharge:** The emotion moves through your body. You cry, you shake, you make sound, you move. Energy discharges.
- **Integration:** The intensity subsides. Your nervous system begins to settle. You can think clearly again.
- **Resolution:** The emotion completes. You feel a sense of relief, release, softening, or settling. Something has moved through and finished.

Trauma interrupts this cycle most commonly at step three, expression and discharge. The emotion activates, reaches peak intensity, and then you suppress it. You swallow it. You push it down. You tighten your muscles and hold your breath and force it underground. The cycle stops mid-stream.

Your body then remains in a state of partial activation, waiting for completion. The unfinished emotion becomes chronic tension, chronic anxiety, chronic numbness, depending on which emotion was interrupted and how you learned to suppress it.

Completing a cycle addresses that specific episode; other emotions may resurface when needed. Sadness isn't something you "finish" once and for all. Anger will arise again when boundaries are violated. What completion means is that *this particular instance* of the emotion, the anger from that specific moment, the fear from that particular event, gets to move through and finish its cycle. You release this piece, even though there may be others.

The practice of emotional completion requires two things: expression and witness.

Expression means allowing the emotion to move through your body in whatever way it wants to, within safe containers. This might be crying, making sound, moving your body, hitting a pillow, writing, creating art. The key is that the emotion gets to express itself in some form rather than remaining held.

Witness means someone (including your own aware self) is present for the emotion without trying to fix it, stop it, or make it go away. The witness simply holds space: "I see you. I'm here. This matters."

Often, the reason emotions couldn't complete in childhood was the absence of a witness. You cried and no one came. You raged and were punished. You trembled and were told to stop being dramatic. The emotion had nowhere to land, no one to receive it, so it stayed incomplete.

Now, as an adult, you can provide that witness for yourself. You can be present for your own emotional experience in a way no one was present for you then. This is the heart of healing: finally being seen, even if you're the one doing the seeing.

When an emotion completes, you'll feel it. There's a tangible shift: a sense of release or relief, physical softening (jaw relaxes, shoulders drop, breath deepens), a feeling of being more present and less activated, sometimes fatigue (discharge takes energy), sometimes clarity (you can think more clearly, see the situation differently), and a sense that something has moved or shifted inside you.

Work in increments. Small pieces add up over time. You can complete small pieces, this morning's frustration, yesterday's sadness, the fear from that memory that surfaced last night. Each small completion contributes to your overall healing. The goal is emotional fluidity: feeling, letting move, completing, and returning to regulation. Your body has been waiting for this permission. It's been waiting for you to be safe enough, resourced enough, and ready enough to finally feel what couldn't be felt. When you give that permission, in small, manageable doses, your body knows exactly what to do. It knows how to complete what was interrupted. It knows how to release what's been held. It knows how to heal.

---

### EXERCISE: Emotion Completion Practice

---

**Step 1:** Choose a recent moment (last few days) when you had to suppress an emotion. Choose something manageable, not your deepest trauma.

The situation: ______________________________________________________________

______________________________________________________________________________

**Step 2:** The emotion I suppressed: ☐ Anger ☐ Sadness ☐ Fear ☐ Frustration

I had to suppress it because: __________________________________________________

______________________________________________________________________________

**Step 3:** Find privacy. Give yourself permission to express it now for 30-90 seconds.

*For anger:* Make fists, tense your body, say the words, hit a pillow, make sounds.

*For sadness:* Let your face show it, let tears come, make sounds of grief.

*For fear:* Let yourself shake or tremble, make yourself small if needed, acknowledge "I was scared."

After expression, place hand on heart. Take three breaths.

Say to yourself: *"I see this. I'm here for this. It's okay to feel this."*

**Step 4:** Did something shift, soften, or release? ☐ Yes ☐ No ☐ A little

How my body feels now compared to before: _______________________________________

______________________________________________________________________________

What I learned: _________________________________________________________________

______________________________________________________________________________

## Your Words Could Change Everything

*"In helping others heal, we deepen our own healing." — Bessel van der Kolk*

Remember how you felt before starting this workbook? The exhaustion of trying everything. The confusion about why your body wouldn't let go. The lonely fear that maybe healing wasn't possible for you.

Right now, someone feels exactly that way. They're scrolling through Amazon at 2am, desperate for relief, reading reviews to find proof that hope isn't foolish.

You can be that proof.

Your honest review, just a few sentences about what you've experienced so far, could be the moment they finally believe healing is possible. I'm grateful for all feedback, positive or negative, and I read every review personally.

Sixty seconds of your time might save someone years of searching.

You know how much finding the right resource matters. Please help someone else find theirs.

Thank you.

# Chapter 7:
# Feeling Away Your Chronic Pain and Illness

*"Pain is inevitable. Suffering is optional. But so is being present for your pain."*
*— Adaptation of Buddhist saying*

What if your pain isn't something to fix, but something to listen to? You've tried everything. The medications that made you foggy without touching the ache. The physical therapy that improved nothing. The specialists who ran every test, looked at every scan, and found exactly nothing wrong. Yet your body still screams. The pain is real. It's there when you wake up, when you try to work, when you attempt to sleep. It shapes every decision, limits every plan, colors every moment of your day.

And somewhere along the way, someone implied it might be in your head. Maybe they didn't say it directly. Maybe it was just the look when the tests came back clear again. The suggestion to "try meditation" or "reduce stress" delivered with a sympathetic smile that felt like dismissal. The unspoken question hanging in the exam room: if we can't find it, does it really exist?

Here's what you need to know: your pain is real. Full stop. Pain that has no visible cause on an MRI is still pain. Symptoms that don't fit neatly into a diagnosis are still symptoms. Your body is not lying to you.

But what if there's another way to understand what's happening? Not instead of the medical explanations you've heard, but alongside them. What if your body is speaking in the only language it has left, and the pain is actually a message you haven't yet learned to decode?

This chapter isn't about blaming you for your pain. It's not suggesting that trauma "causes" every physical symptom or that you've somehow created your illness through unresolved emotions. The relationship between mind and body is far more complex than simple cause and effect.

What this chapter offers is a different lens. For some people with chronic pain, particularly pain that doesn't respond to conventional treatment, there's often a nervous system component. Your brain, trying desperately to protect you, may have learned to generate pain as an alarm system. And that alarm system, sensitized by trauma, might now be stuck in the "on" position, creating real physical sensations even when there's no tissue damage to repair.

If this describes your experience, then pushing harder against your symptoms, seeking the next treatment, trying to force your body into submission, these strategies might actually be keeping you trapped. What if the way out isn't through more resistance, but through listening? Through feeling toward your pain rather than running from it?

This approach won't resonate with everyone. Some chronic pain has clear physical origins that require medical intervention. Some illnesses need pharmaceutical management. But if you've tried everything else and you're still hurting, if your pain seems to have a life of its own that medical science can't quite explain, then what you'll learn here might change everything.

Your body has been trying to tell you something. Maybe it's time to listen.

## When Pain Is a Message Your Body Needs You to Hear

Sarah's back pain started the week her father died. A sharp, burning sensation that seized her lower spine and wouldn't let go. She saw orthopedists, tried physical therapy, got imaging done. The MRI showed mild disc degeneration, the kind almost everyone her age has, nothing that explained the intensity of her pain. But the pain persisted. For three years, it shaped her life. She stopped exercising, changed jobs, arranged her entire existence around this fire in her spine.

Then one day, working with a therapist on her grief, something shifted. As she finally allowed herself to feel the weight of her father's death, to cry the tears she'd been holding back, the back pain began to fade. Within weeks, it was gone.

Was the pain fake? No. Was it "all in her head"? Absolutely not. Sarah's pain was as real as a broken bone. But its source wasn't structural damage. It was her nervous system, overwhelmed by grief it couldn't process, speaking in the only language it knew: sensation.

This is neuroplastic pain. Pain generated not by tissue damage, but by the brain itself.

Your brain is designed to create pain. That's not a flaw; it's a feature. Pain is your body's alarm system, designed to alert you to danger so you can protect yourself. Touch a hot stove, and pain pulls your hand back before you think. Twist your ankle, and pain stops you from walking on it while it heals. This is acute pain: useful, protective, temporary.

But sometimes the alarm system gets stuck. The brain learns to produce pain even after the original injury heals, or in response to emotional threats instead of physical ones. Central sensitization happens when your nervous system becomes so sensitive that normal sensations get amplified into pain signals. The volume dial gets turned up and won't turn back down.

Here's what makes this particularly relevant for those who lived in prolonged stress: trauma sensitizes your pain pathways. When your nervous system has spent years in survival mode, it becomes hypervigilant about everything, including physical sensations.

You might notice this in your own body: • Pain that moves from one area to another. • Pain that worsens with stress but not with exertion. • Pain that lessens when you feel calm or connected.

Each of these suggests your nervous system is involved in the experience.

Think about it this way: acute pain signals danger. It says, "Something is wrong right now, fix it." But chronic neuroplastic pain IS the danger signal. The pain itself is the alarm, blaring long after the original threat has passed. Your body, unable to complete the protective responses that trauma interrupted, unable to process the emotions it wasn't safe to feel, converts all that unfinished business into physical sensation.

Pain becomes compressed emotion. The grief Sarah couldn't let herself feel. The anger that was too dangerous to express. The fear that had nowhere to go. When feelings can't move through you, when protective responses get frozen mid-action, when needs go unmet for so long you forget you have them, all of that gets stored. And sometimes, it gets stored as pain.

This doesn't mean your pain is imaginary or that you can just think it away. Neuroplastic pain is created by real neural pathways, real brain changes, real nervous system dysregulation. But it does mean something crucial: if your brain learned to create this pain, it can learn to turn it down. If the pain is a message, you can learn to hear what it's trying to tell you.

Not all chronic pain is neuroplastic. Some pain has clear structural causes that need medical treatment. But if your pain fits the patterns above, if it started during a stressful period, if it's disproportionate to any findings on tests, these are clues that your nervous system might be involved. And if your nervous system is involved, then you have more power than you think. Because unlike structural damage, neural pathways can change. The brain that learned to create pain can learn something new.

### EXERCISE: Pain as Communication

Place a hand over the painful area. Feel its shape, warmth, or pressure. Notice what it's like to bring gentle attention here.

Now ask it these questions and write whatever comes, without filtering:

What are you trying to tell me?

What are you protecting me from?

What do you need me to know?

This isn't about getting "correct" answers. You're opening dialogue with your body's wisdom. Return to this when pain intensifies to notice emerging patterns.

## The Link Between Unprocessed Trauma and Physical Symptoms

Research confirms what Sarah's story suggests: trauma lives in the body in measurable, physical ways.

Adults who experienced four or more Adverse Childhood Experiences are twice as likely to develop heart disease, four times as likely to develop chronic lung disease, and twelve times as likely to attempt suicide. They have significantly higher rates of autoimmune disorders, chronic pain conditions, fibromyalgia, chronic fatigue syndrome, irritable bowel syndrome, and unexplained medical symptoms.

This isn't coincidence. This is your body keeping the score.

When you experience trauma, especially chronic developmental trauma, your body mounts a stress response. Cortisol floods your system. Inflammation increases. Your immune system goes on high alert. If the trauma is temporary, these systems reset. But if trauma becomes your normal, if childhood means constant threat, if years pass in survival mode, these emergency responses become your baseline.

Your body was never designed to run at this level of activation continuously. Chronic stress becomes chronic inflammation.

You might notice this even now. Your shoulders tense, your breath shortens. These are echoes of the same system that learned to brace years ago.

Chronic inflammation damages tissues, disrupts healing, dysregulates immune function. Your body, pumping out stress hormones year after year, paying the metabolic cost of constant vigilance, eventually shows the wear.

This is the body burden of unprocessed trauma. Not abstract psychological impact, but literal physiological cost. Your cardiovascular system stressed beyond its design limits. Your digestive system disrupted by a gut-brain axis in constant alarm. Your immune system so overactivated that it starts attacking your own tissues, autoimmune conditions that mirror, in your cells, the way trauma taught you to turn against yourself.

Chronic trauma often appears through the body as: • Persistent muscle tension without injury. • Digestive distress linked to emotional stress. • Exhaustion that rest doesn't resolve. • Autoimmune flare-ups during emotional overwhelm. • Headaches or migraines in periods of high alert.

The gut-brain connection is particularly revealing. Your digestive system contains more neurotransmitters than your brain. It's often called your "second brain," and it's in constant communication with your central nervous system. When your nervous system registers threat, your digestion shuts down. Blood flow redirects to muscles for fighting or fleeing, digestive processes pause. This makes perfect sense if you're running from a predator. It makes no sense if you're sitting in class, lying in bed, or eating dinner, but your body still thinks you're in danger.

Do this for years, and you get IBS, chronic nausea, mysterious food sensitivities, conditions that puzzle gastroenterologists because the structural tests show nothing wrong. The problem isn't in your intestines. It's in the conversation between your gut and your hypervigilant nervous system.

Fibromyalgia tells a similar story. Widespread pain and fatigue with no clear structural cause, disproportionately affecting those who experienced childhood adversity. The pain is real, brain imaging shows altered pain processing, but it's not tissue damage. It's a nervous system that learned to amplify danger signals, that never learned to turn down the volume after the threat passed.

Chronic fatigue syndrome, with its crushing exhaustion that no amount of rest fixes. Autoimmune conditions where the body attacks itself, as if your cells learned the same self-directed hostility that trauma taught your psyche. Chronic migraines, temporomandibular joint disorder, interstitial cystitis, chronic pelvic pain, conditions that cluster in people who grew up unsafe at rates far beyond chance.

The research is clear: childhood adversity predicts adult illness. The more types of trauma you experienced, the higher your risk.

This isn't abstract data. It's lived reality inside bodies that never got to rest.

But here's what's crucial: understanding this connection doesn't mean you caused your illness. You didn't choose trauma. You didn't decide to have a hypervigilant nervous system. You didn't give yourself fibromyalgia by failing to process your emotions correctly. Your body did exactly what bodies do under prolonged threat, it adapted to survive.

The question isn't, "Why did I create this?" The question is, "Now that I understand what my body has been carrying, what becomes possible?"

Because if trauma contributed to these conditions, then trauma healing might address them in ways conventional medicine can't. If your nervous system learned these patterns, it can learn new ones. If your body has been working overtime to protect you, and that work created these physical costs, then teaching your body it's finally safe might change everything.

This isn't magical thinking. It's neuroscience. Neural pathways are plastic, they change based on experience. Your body's stress response can be retrained. Inflammation can decrease when your nervous system downregulates. Immune function can stabilize when you're no longer living in constant alarm.

Understanding the trauma-illness connection doesn't give you a simple cure. But it gives you something potentially more valuable: a roadmap. A way to understand why conventional treatments might have failed. A reason to believe that addressing trauma could improve physical symptoms. A framework that makes your body's struggles make sense.

Your body isn't broken. It's been doing exactly what it was designed to do under impossible circumstances. Now you can help it learn a different way.

EXERCISE: My Body's Timeline

Draw a simple timeline from birth to present. Above the line, mark traumatic events or difficult periods. Below the line, mark when physical symptoms began.

Birth ______________________________________________________________________ Present

**Patterns I Notice:**

Do certain symptoms cluster around certain times?

________________________________________________________________________________

Did symptoms emerge during trauma or after?

________________________________________________________________________________

What surprises me about this timeline?

________________________________________________________________________________

Remember: This isn't about proving causation. You're noticing connections your body might be showing you.

## Listening to Your Pain Instead of Fighting It

You've probably spent years negotiating with your body through resistance instead of relationship. Pushing through pain, distracting from it, medicating it away, tensing against it. This makes perfect sense. Pain hurts. Resistance seems like the only logical response.

But what if resistance is actually amplifying the signal?

The cycle works like this: • Pain triggers fear. • Fear activates the nervous system. • Tension increases pain.

Breaking the loop begins with calming the fear, not fighting the sensation.

Here's the paradox: pain plus resistance equals suffering. The pain itself is sensation, unpleasant, yes, but just sensation. The suffering comes from what you add to it. The story you tell about it. The fear of what it means. The desperate wish for it to be different. The constant battle to make it go away.

Sensation by itself is tolerable. It's the story around it that becomes unbearable.

Resistance keeps your nervous system in threat mode. When you fight pain, you signal to your brain that the pain is dangerous, which reinforces the exact neural pathways that generate the pain in the first place. You create the very thing you're trying to escape.

What if there's another way?

Turning toward your pain instead of away from it sounds absurd. Counterintuitive. Maybe even masochistic. But this isn't about enjoying pain or tolerating unnecessary suffering. It's about changing your relationship with sensation in a way that actually reduces the threat signal.

Think about quicksand. Struggle violently and you sink faster. The harder you fight, the more stuck you become. But stillness, counterintuitive, scary stillness, actually allows you to float. Movement becomes possible again, but only after you stop the desperate thrashing.

Pain works similarly. When you stop fighting sensation and start observing it with curiosity instead of fear, something shifts in your nervous system. The amygdala stops screaming alarm. The prefrontal cortex comes back online. Your body receives a different message: "I can handle this. This isn't an emergency. I'm safe even with this sensation present."

This is not passive resignation. This is not giving up on healing or accepting that you'll hurt forever. This is active engagement, meeting your experience exactly as it is rather than exhausting yourself trying to make it something else.

Acceptance doesn't mean you want the pain or think it's good. It means you stop adding the layer of suffering that comes from constant resistance. You feel what you feel without the additional weight of wishing it away every single moment.

The difference is crucial. Passive resignation sounds like, "I guess I'll just hurt forever and there's nothing I can do." Active acceptance sounds like, "Right now, in this moment, this is what I feel. I can be present with this. I can explore what this sensation actually is without the story of catastrophe."

When you stop treating pain as an enemy, when you bring curiosity instead of fear, your nervous system receives proof that the sensation isn't actually dangerous. Over time, this can create the very change that fighting prevented. Because your brain, constantly scanning for threat, learns that these sensations don't require an alarm response.

Will the pain disappear instantly? Probably not. But it might soften. It might become more bearable. You might discover that you have more capacity to be with discomfort than you thought. And in that space between stimulus and suffering, something new becomes possible.

The goal is to rebuild communication. Because the way forward is through direct experience, not resistance.

**EXERCISE: Pain Observation Practice**

Set a timer for 3 minutes. Choose one area of pain and observe it like a scientist gathering data, not trying to change anything.

*What's the quality? (sharp, dull, burning, aching, throbbing)*

---------------------------------------------------------------------------------------

*Where exactly is it located?*

---------------------------------------------------------------------------------------

*Does it move or stay still?*

---------------------------------------------------------------------------------------

*What happens when you breathe toward this area?*

---------------------------------------------------------------------------------------

*Did anything shift during these 3 minutes?*

---------------------------------------------------------------------------------------

After three minutes, stretch gently and notice if your posture wants to adjust. You're training your nervous system that you can be present with sensation without catastrophe.

## Somatic Tracking to Transform Your Relationship With Discomfort

Alan Gordon, founder of Pain Reprocessing Therapy, discovered something remarkable: you can retrain your brain's response to pain by changing how you pay attention to it. The technique is called somatic tracking, a way of paying attention to pain with curiosity instead of fear. It works by interrupting the fear response that amplifies pain signals.

Here's the basic principle: your brain generates pain when it perceives danger. For chronic pain, especially neuroplastic pain, the danger isn't in your tissues, it's in your brain's interpretation of sensations. Your amygdala learned that certain sensations mean threat, so it amplifies the alarm. Somatic tracking retrains that response by teaching your brain that sensation doesn't equal danger.

The practice has three core components: attention, curiosity, and safety.

First, you bring your attention directly to the painful sensation. Not avoiding it, not distracting from it, but focusing on it with the same scientific interest you'd give to any other phenomenon. You're studying the sensation itself, separate from the meaning you've assigned to it.

Second, you approach the sensation with genuine curiosity rather than fear or judgment. Not "Oh no, here it is again," but "Interesting, what exactly is this sensation right now?" You're investigating texture, location, quality, as if you're encountering it for the first time.

Third, and most crucially, you pair this attention with messages of safety. While you're feeling the pain, you consciously remind yourself: "I'm okay. This is just sensation. My body is safe. This feeling isn't dangerous, it's just my nervous system being protective." You're literally speaking to your amygdala, telling it to stand down. You might notice subtle signs of safety even now, a longer breath, softer shoulders, a hint of calm returning. This combination creates neuroplastic change. Your brain starts to learn that these sensations aren't emergencies. The pain signal, no longer amplified by fear, begins to decrease. Over time, sometimes remarkably quickly, chronic pain can shift or even resolve completely.

This doesn't work for all pain. If you have structural damage that needs medical attention, somatic tracking won't heal broken bones. But for pain driven by nervous system sensitization, for symptoms that have outlasted any original injury, for discomfort that seems disproportionate to medical findings, this approach can be transformative.

Here's the step-by-step protocol:

- Start by finding the exact location of your pain. Get specific, not just "my back hurts" but exactly where, exactly what kind of sensation.
- Describe the sensation in purely sensory terms. Avoid emotional words like "terrible" or "unbearable." Just the facts: sharp, dull, burning, pressing, whatever you actually feel.
- Bring curiosity to the experience. Say to yourself, "Interesting, this is what pain feels like right now." Notice if the sensation changes even slightly as you observe it.
- Send explicit safety messages to your nervous system. "I'm okay. My body is safe. This sensation doesn't mean danger. My brain is just being protective, but I'm actually safe right now."
- Notice any shifts, no matter how subtle. Does the pain intensity change? Does it move? Does the quality shift? Sometimes the changes are tiny at first, honor them anyway.
- Find one neutral or pleasant sensation somewhere else in your body. The feeling of your feet on the floor. The coolness of breath in your nostrils. The softness of fabric on your skin. Anything that isn't painful.
- Alternate your attention between the painful sensation and the neutral one. Spend 30 seconds with pain, with curiosity and safety, then 30 seconds with the neutral sensation. Back and forth.

This last step is crucial. It teaches your brain that not everything in your body is a threat. It builds a wider capacity range where pain isn't the only thing screaming for attention. It demonstrates that you can shift focus, which itself is a form of control.

Practice this for five minutes at a time. Don't expect miracles immediately. This is retraining neural pathways that have been established for months or years. But with consistent practice, many people experience significant reduction in pain intensity, frequency, or both. The key is genuine curiosity and safety. If you're doing this while secretly still terrified of the pain, while still desperately wanting it to disappear, your nervous system will pick up on that fear and stay in alarm mode. This practice requires a light touch, interested, gentle, almost playful. "Huh, look at that. My body is doing this interesting thing. I'm safe enough to just observe it." You're teaching your brain a new language. Pain doesn't have to mean danger. Sensation doesn't require emergency response. You can feel what you feel and be okay. That lesson, repeated over time, can change everything.

---

### EXERCISE: Somatic Tracking Protocol

---

**Instructions:**

1. Choose one area of pain
2. Locate exactly where the sensation is
3. Describe the quality in sensory terms only (not "terrible," just "sharp" or "burning")
4. Say aloud or silently: "Interesting, this is what this feels like right now"
5. Send safety aloud: "I'm okay. My body is safe. This is sensation, not danger"
6. Notice any shifts in intensity or quality
7. Find one neutral sensation elsewhere (feet on floor, breath, fabric on skin)
8. Alternate: 30 seconds on pain (with curiosity), 30 seconds on neutral sensation
9. Continue for 5 minutes

**Track your experience:**

Location:________________________________________Quality:___________________________________

Starting intensity (1-10): ______ Ending intensity (1-10): ______

What shifted? _____________________________________________________________________________

Practice daily. You're retraining neural pathways, consistency matters more than immediate results.

## Moving Through Pain With Compassion and Curiosity

When your body hurts, every instinct tells you to stay still. To protect the painful area, guard it, avoid movement that might make things worse. This makes sense for acute injury, don't walk on a broken ankle. But for chronic pain, especially pain driven by nervous system sensitization, immobility often becomes part of the problem. Your brain needs information. Movement provides that information. When you move a body part and nothing terrible happens, when you use muscles and joints and they function, you're sending your brain proof that your body is safe and capable. You're demonstrating that movement doesn't equal damage.

This is particularly important for those whose bodies learned to brace against threat. Chronic muscle tension, guarding patterns, protective holding, these were necessary once. They kept you safe. But sustained over years, they create their own pain. Tight muscles ache. Restricted movement causes compensation patterns. Your body, frozen in defensive postures, starts to hurt from the very strategies it used to protect itself. Gentle movement becomes medicine. Not aggressive exercise that forces through pain, but compassionate exploration that works with your body's current capacity. You're looking for the edge where challenge meets safety, where movement is possible without injury.

There's an important distinction here: "good hurt" versus "bad hurt." Good hurt is sensation that challenges you but doesn't harm you, the stretch that feels intense but not stabbing, the movement that's effortful but not injurious. Bad hurt is sharp, protective, your body's clear signal to stop. Learning to distinguish between them is crucial. For many people who grew up in survival mode, all discomfort gets labeled as danger. Your threat detection system can't tell the difference between challenging sensation and harmful sensation because it's been in alarm mode so long that everything feels like emergency. Relearning this distinction, "I can feel this and be okay; this sensation means effort, not injury," is part of recalibrating your nervous system.

Start small. Ridiculously small. If your neck hurts, try the tiniest rotation, just degrees, not full range. If your back aches, try the slightest pelvic tilt. You're not trying to achieve anything; you're gathering information. Can I move here? What happens when I do? Where's the edge of okay?

Compassionate self-touch can amplify this work. Placing a gentle hand on a painful area while you move it sends multiple safety signals: your own touch provides proprioceptive input that can calm the nervous system; the warmth and pressure of your hand offers comfort; your conscious attention demonstrates that you're caring for this body part rather than treating it as territory to conquer.

This matters more than it might seem. Trauma often involves a severed relationship with your body, it hurt you, it betrayed you, it became dangerous territory. Every moment of compassionate touch, every instance of gentle movement with care rather than force, rebuilds that relationship. You're demonstrating to your body that you're no longer negotiating through resistance.

The practice is simple: choose an area that holds pain. If you can reach it comfortably, place your hand there with gentle pressure. Speak to this area, out loud or silently, whichever feels less absurd. "I'm sorry you hurt. I'm here with you. I'm not going to force you or ignore you. Let's see what's possible."

Then move. Slowly. Gently. Exploring range of motion not to achieve anything but to discover what's here. Can this shoulder roll forward a little? What about back? Where does the discomfort increase? Where's the zone where I feel sensation but not emergency?

You're practicing titration, going right to the edge of your capacity without exceeding it. This is how your nervous system learns to expand its zone of safety. You prove you can handle some discomfort without catastrophe, and gradually, "some" becomes "more."

This work complements medical treatment; it doesn't replace it. If you need physical therapy, medication, or other interventions, use them. Somatic approaches aren't instead of conventional medicine, they're alongside it. You're adding tools to your toolkit, not throwing out the tools you already have. What you're doing here is more than pain management. You're changing your relationship with your body from adversarial to collaborative. You're teaching your nervous system that movement is safe, that sensation can be tolerated, that your body is capable of more than you thought. You're demonstrating, in the most concrete way possible, that you're no longer under threat.

Some days, movement will feel impossible. Some days, pain will win. That's okay. This isn't about forcing yourself into wellness or pushing through every limit. It's about the moments when you can explore, when you can move with kindness rather than fear, when you can touch your body with compassion rather than resentment.

Those moments accumulate. Those moments teach your nervous system a new story. And gradually, sometimes so slowly you barely notice, sometimes in sudden shifts that feel like miracles, your body starts to believe it. Sarah didn't just lose her back pain; she gained a new relationship with her body. Each act of gentle movement tells your nervous system a new story: you are safe now. You can move and still be whole. Your body remembers how to trust again.

---

### EXERCISE: Compassionate Movement Exploration

---

**Instructions:**

1. Choose one area that holds pain
2. Place a gentle hand there if you can reach it
3. Say: "I'm sorry you hurt. I'm here with you"
4. Move the area very slowly and gently (rotate, flex, rock, circle)
5. Notice where the edge of comfortable movement is
6. Practice moving with kindness, not force, for 3-5 minutes

**What I discovered:**

Can I move through this pain? ____________________________________________

Where's the edge of okay? ________________________________________________

What's the difference between "good hurt" and "bad hurt" here?

______________________________________________________________________

What happens when I move with compassion instead of force?

______________________________________________________________________

Practice this daily. You're rebuilding trust with your body, one gentle movement at a time.

# Chapter 8:
# Meeting Your Inner Parts Through IFS

*"You are not a mess. You are a feeling person in a messy world." — Glennon Doyle*

One part of you wants to open up and trust. Another part slams the door shut. One part longs for connection. Another part pushes everyone away. One part wants to heal. Another part says it's not safe yet.

You are multiple. Your inner life organizes itself in parts.

Right now, you might be feeling that internal tug-of-war. The voice that says "try harder" battles the voice that says "give up." The part that craves intimacy fights the part that needs distance. You may feel this pull in your chest or stomach, the body holding both forward and back at once. You've probably judged yourself for these contradictions, called yourself inconsistent, accused yourself of self-sabotage.

What if these aren't contradictions at all? What if they're parts: distinct sub-personalities, each with their own history, their own fears, their own job to do?

These opposing pulls are not only thoughts. They live as muscle tension, shifts in breath, and protective postures your body learned long ago.

Internal Family Systems offers a paradigm shift. The voices inside you signal complexity, not pathology. Your psyche organized itself this way to survive. Every part, even the ones you hate, is trying to help. The anxious part that keeps you up at night? It's protecting you from being blindsided. The numb part that shuts down your feelings? It's preventing overwhelm. A critical voice tries to keep you within rules it believes will prevent rejection.

Multiplicity is part of being human. Trauma amplifies and polarizes this natural system.

As you learn to listen instead of control, the conflict between your parts can become collaboration.

This chapter invites you to meet your inner family with curiosity instead of judgment. You'll learn why you have these different voices, what they're protecting, and how to become the calm, compassionate leader they've been waiting for. You'll discover that beneath all the noise, there's a Self (your true essence) that remains intact beneath everything that happened.

Your parts carry solutions that need your leadership. They just need you to understand what they've been trying to tell you all along.

## Why You Have Different Parts Inside You

You know that feeling when you want two opposite things at the same time? When you're standing at the threshold of something new and part of you is excited while another part is terrified? When you promise yourself you'll set a boundary and then the moment arrives and you fold?

That's multiplicity.

Your mind is naturally multiple. It always has been. You have parts: sub-personalities with their own feelings, beliefs, memories, and agendas. A planner that needs control, a child that seeks comfort, a critic that demands perfection, a dreamer that hopes for more. These inner figures formed to help you adapt to life's contradictions.

One part holds your anger. Another holds your sadness. One part wants to be seen. Another part wants to hide. One part believes you're capable. Another part believes you'll fail.

Internal Family Systems theory says multiplicity is how your mind organizes complexity. At work you organize and perform; with friends you soften and play. Each part carries a role appropriate to its context. You have a part that's responsible, and a part that's spontaneous. These aren't masks you wear. They're genuine aspects of who you are.

The challenge isn't having parts. The challenge is what happens when trauma forces those parts into extreme roles.

When you experience trauma (especially developmental trauma, especially repeated trauma) your parts go into crisis mode. They stop working together as a team and start working against each other. Some lock away the pain so you can function. Others stand guard to keep it from surfacing. The system becomes polarized, pulling in opposite directions.

Notice where you feel this push and pull right now. Shoulders. Jaw. Belly.

This tension is your system's way of keeping balance between protection and desire.

Here's what matters: beneath all those parts, there's a core Self. Your calm, compassionate leadership inside. It's the part of you that's calm when parts are anxious. Curious when parts are judgmental. Compassionate when parts are harsh. Confident when parts are insecure.

Self remains intact beneath everything that happened. Parts can be wounded, exiled, frozen in time. But Self is always there, waiting beneath the noise.

The goal is to help parts relax their extreme roles and let Self lead. When Self is in charge, parts don't have to work so hard. The protectors can step back. The wounded ones can be heard. The system finds balance.

Parts express multiple intentions within continuous awareness, while dissociation interrupts awareness itself.

Your system learned protective strategies that made sense at the time. Trauma makes parts more extreme, more rigid, more desperate. But multiplicity itself was already there. You were designed this way. Your parts are how you process complexity, how you hold conflicting truths, how you adapt to different contexts.

The relief comes when you stop trying to be one unified, consistent person and start recognizing the different voices inside you. When you stop saying "I'm such a mess, I can't even figure out what I want" and start saying "My anxious part wants safety, and my adventurous part wants growth, and they're both valid."

Your contradictions make sense. Different parts developed in different contexts, learned different lessons, came to different conclusions. The part that trusts people learned that lesson from someone safe. The part that doesn't trust learned that lesson from someone dangerous. Both are telling the truth about their experience.

When you understand this, the internal tension can begin to ease. You're learning to listen to all of them and lead from a place that honors what each one knows.

When you lead from Self, inner conflict becomes communication.

---

## ✎ EXERCISE: Identifying My Parts

---

Complete these prompts to begin naming your parts:

*The part of me that feels anxious wants:*

____________________________________________________________________________________

*The part of me that gets angry is protecting:*

____________________________________________________________________________________

*The part of me that shuts down is afraid of:*

____________________________________________________________________________________

*The part of me that wants to heal believes:*

____________________________________________________________________________________

*Notes: Other parts I notice*

____________________________________________________________________________________

____________________________________________________________________________________

____________________________________________________________________________________

____________________________________________________________________________________

## Understanding Your Protectors and What They're Guarding

Your protectors are the parts that stepped in when life felt unsafe. They're the ones who said "I'll handle this" when you were too young, too overwhelmed, too alone to handle it yourself. They stepped in. They took over. They've been working overtime ever since. Every protector has a style.

There are two types of protectors in your system, and they have completely different strategies.

Managers are protective parts that try to prevent pain through control. They're the planners, the worriers, the perfectionists. They're the part that wakes you up at 3 a.m. running through worst-case scenarios. They're the part that says "if I can just be good enough, smart enough, helpful enough, I'll be safe." They're the part that people-pleases, overworks, stays hypervigilant, never lets you rest.

Managers focus on control because control once meant safety.

Managers believe that if they can control everything, you'll never have to feel that pain again. They manage your image, your relationships, your environment. They scan for threats. They avoid vulnerability. They keep you busy so you don't have time to feel.

Then there are the Firefighters. These are protective parts that try to stop pain fast through distraction or numbing. They show up when the feelings break through anyway (when the Managers' prevention strategies fail and you're flooded with emotion). Firefighters don't prevent the fire. They put it out. Fast. By any means necessary.

Firefighters are the parts that numb, distract, escape. They're the binge eating, the substance use, the dissociation, the rage, the self-harm, the compulsive scrolling, the risky behavior. They're the part that says "I can't feel this" and does whatever it takes to make the feeling stop. They're trying to save you from drowning in pain you don't have the resources to process.

The urgency they bring can feel chaotic, but in their logic it's rescue.

You might notice protectors through patterns like:

- Overthinking or constant planning
- People-pleasing or perfectionism
- Emotional numbing or overindulgence or escape behavior
- Explosive anger or sudden withdrawal
- Harsh self-criticism that tries to keep you acceptable

Your Managers and Firefighters are often at odds. The Manager says "control yourself, be disciplined, don't mess up." The Firefighter says "I don't care, I just need relief." The Manager judges the Firefighter for being destructive. The Firefighter resents the Manager for being so rigid. But they're both protectors. They're both trying to keep you safe.

Living between tight control and quick escape is exhausting. Both are trying to keep you safe with the tools they learned. What are they protecting? They're guarding the exiled parts: young, burdened parts that carry pain and beliefs from the past.

Imagine a child who learned that showing vulnerability leads to punishment. A Manager part develops: "I'll make sure we're never vulnerable again. I'll be perfect. I'll control everything." Now imagine that same person in adulthood, facing a situation where perfection isn't possible. The feelings start to surface. The Manager can't hold them back. A Firefighter part kicks in: "Drink. Dissociate. Rage. Anything to make this feeling stop."

Both protectors believe they're saving your life. The Manager believes that if it stops controlling, you'll be hurt. The Firefighter believes that if it doesn't numb the pain, you'll be destroyed by it. Their strategies once worked, but the cost of keeping them now is high. They developed these strategies for a reason. They learned these patterns when you actually were too young, too small, too alone to handle what was happening.

A critical part watches for mistakes, believing that constant correction prevents harm. It sounds like the enemy: the voice that says you're not good enough, that you're failing, that everyone sees through you. But it's trying to make you acceptable. It believes that if it can just point out all your flaws first, you can fix them before anyone else notices. It's trying to prevent rejection by keeping you in line. It learned that being "good enough" might keep you safe.

The work is to help protectors see that you're not in that situation anymore. That the strategies that kept you alive then are costing you your life now. That they can step back because there's a Self (your calm, capable, compassionate core) who can handle what they've been carrying alone.

When you develop compassion for your protectors instead of fighting them, something shifts. When you can say "thank you for working so hard to keep me safe" instead of "why can't I just stop doing this," the protectors begin to trust you. They begin to relax. They're exhausted. They've been carrying this burden for years. They want to rest. They just need to know someone else can hold what they've been holding. When your Self stays steady, their work becomes guidance instead of defense.

---

## ✎ EXERCISE: Meeting My Protectors

---

### Part 1: My Manager Part

Managers try to prevent bad things from happening through control, planning, perfecting, pleasing, or achieving.

My Manager shows up as: ________________________________________________

What this part is afraid will happen if it stops: ______________________________

________________________________________________________________

**Part 2: My Firefighter Part**

Firefighters react when emotions become overwhelming through numbing, distracting, or escaping.

My Firefighter shows up as: ________________________________________________________________

What this part is afraid will happen if it stops: __________________________________________________

______________________________________________________________________________________

______________________________________________________________________________________

## Finding the Exiled Parts That Hold Your Pain

Beneath the protectors, hidden behind all that defense, are the exiles.

Exiles are young, burdened parts that carry pain and beliefs from the past. Exiles usually carry burdened beliefs such as "I am bad," "I am unlovable," "It was my fault." These are conclusions drawn in overwhelm. These beliefs formed to make sense of the unbearable and can be updated.

Exiles often carry the original sensations of fear, shame, and loss linked to moments when you felt alone and unprotected.

These are the parts your protectors are desperately trying to keep locked away.

Exiles got their name because they were banished from consciousness. When the pain was too big, too overwhelming, too dangerous to feel, your system made a decision: we can't eliminate this part, but we can exile it. We can lock it in the basement. We can build walls around it. We can make sure it never gets out.

Your Managers guard the door. Your Firefighters fight the flames when the exile starts to break through. The system's priority becomes keeping that pain away from awareness.

But exiles don't stay quietly locked away. When you're triggered, an Exile breaks through. A sound, a tone, or a smell may bring a rush of emotion that belongs to another time.

The protectors couldn't hold it back. The exile is trying to be seen, trying to be heard, trying to tell you what happened.

Sense where this part sits in or around your body. Name the place without trying to change it.

Notice if your body changes temperature, breath, or posture as you name it.

The work with exiles is witnessing and unburdening. You help the exile tell their story to your Self, the compassionate presence who can finally say "I see you. I believe you. It wasn't your fault." You help them release the burdens they've been carrying. You update their beliefs. You let them know the danger is over.

But you can't do this work by force.

Do not bypass protectors. Ask them what proof they need to let you listen.

If you try to access an exile before the protectors are ready, the protectors will create backlash. They'll increase the anxiety, ramp up the defenses, trigger a Firefighter response. They're protecting a part they believe can't survive being felt.

You have to earn the protectors' trust first. You have to let them know you're not going to bypass them, override them, or shame them. You have to show them you can handle what they've been handling. Only then will they allow access to the exiles.

If strong emotions arise, seek the support of a trained IFS or somatic therapist. Exiles carry the core wounds. Approaching them requires safety, pacing, and support.

What you can do now is acknowledge that they exist. You can send a message to the parts of you that have been carrying pain alone: "I know you're there. I see you. I'm not ready to hear your whole story yet, but I'm learning how to be with you. You won't be alone anymore."

That's the beginning: contact without rescue, presence without fixing.

End every contact by saying when you will return. Consistency builds trust.

---

### EXERCISE: Sensing My Exiles

---

Find a quiet space. Close your eyes if that feels safe, or keep a soft gaze downward. Take three deep breaths.

Ask internally: *"Is there a young part of me that's been carrying pain alone?"*

Don't search or force. Just notice what arises.

What I notice:

An image, memory, or feeling: ______________________________________________

________________________________________________________________________

A sense of age or emotion: ________________________________________________

Message to this part:

*"I know you're there. I see you. You're not alone anymore."*

What I want this part to know:

________________________________________________________________________

________________________________________________________________________

*Note: If you felt overwhelmed, that's protectors working. Thank them for protecting you.*

## Accessing Your True Self Beneath the Noise

You've spent so much time listening to parts (the anxious voice, the critical voice, the numb voice) that you might have forgotten there's something else inside you. Something that isn't a part. Something that remains intact beneath everything that happened.

Your Self.

Self isn't created; it's revealed when protection quiets. It's been there all along, beneath the parts. It's the essence of who you are: the calm, clear, compassionate core that exists even in the middle of chaos.

Self has qualities. IFS calls them the 8 C's. When you are in Self, you may notice:

- Calm: shoulders settle, breath widens
- Curiosity: questions arise without pressure
- Compassion: warmth in tone toward the part
- Confidence: a quiet yes in the chest
- Creativity: images or options appear on their own
- Clarity: fewer words, simpler choices
- Courage: willingness to stay present
- Connection: a felt link to yourself and others

These qualities emerge naturally as parts relax. You don't create them; you recognize them.

When you're in Self, you feel spacious instead of tight. Grounded instead of scattered. Open instead of defended. You're present. You're not rushing to fix or change anything. You're just here.

Parts don't have these qualities. Parts feel anxious, judgmental, numb, angry, desperate. Parts have agendas (they want something to happen or not happen). Self doesn't have an agenda. Self just is.

Think about a moment when you felt genuinely compassionate toward someone. Maybe you comforted a child. Maybe you listened to a friend without trying to fix them. Maybe you looked at an animal or stood in nature and felt connected to something bigger. That was Self. You couldn't name it, but you were there.

Self remains intact beneath everything that happened. Trauma can wound parts (exile them, freeze them, push them into extreme roles). But Self is like the quiet room inside the house. Noise can pass by. The room remains available.

You can visit this room for moments. The more often you return, the easier it becomes to find.

The challenge is that parts often blend with you so completely that you think you are them. The anxious part blends and suddenly you're not noticing anxiety, you are anxiety. The critical part blends and you're not hearing criticism, you are the critic. The numb part blends and you're not experiencing numbness, you are numb.

The key to accessing Self is getting parts to unblend, even just slightly.

Ask one question to check who is leading: "How do I feel toward this part?" Curiosity means Self is present. Judgment means another part is leading.

If the answer is compassion, curiosity, calm, that's Self. If the answer is judgment, frustration, fear, impatience, that's another part. A part is judging the part you're trying to work with.

When that happens, you ask the judging part to step back. Not to leave. Not to be eliminated. Just to step back a little so you can see from Self. You keep asking until you feel even a hint of curiosity or compassion. That shift (from judgment to curiosity) is the toggle from part to Self.

You can practice this toggle anytime. Notice a part. Check: "How do I feel toward this part?" If it's judgment, ask that part to step back. Keep checking. Eventually you'll feel the shift. It might be subtle (just a softening, a breath, a sense of space). That's Self.

Self is a presence that appears in moments and grows with practice. Those moments are enough. When parts experience being witnessed by Self (even briefly) they begin to change. They don't need to be fixed. They need to be seen.

You access Self by inviting parts to relax, to trust, to let you lead. They've been leading because no one else could. When they see that Self can handle what they've been handling, they can finally rest.

Even if you rarely feel calm or compassionate, the fact that you're curious about this process means Self is already present.

Your parts have been waiting for this. They've been running the system because they thought no one else could. When Self shows up, when they feel your presence, they can stop working so hard. They can let you take the lead.

That's what this work is: helping Self step forward so the parts can finally step back.

---

## EXERCISE: Calling Forth Self

---

Think of a part you struggle with (your inner critic, anxious part, numb part, people-pleasing part).

The part I'm working with: ______________________________________________

**Step 1:** Ask yourself: *"How do I feel toward this part right now?"*

My honest answer: ______________________________________________

**Step 2:** If your answer is judgment, frustration, fear, or impatience, that's another part.

Say internally: *"I see you. Would you be willing to step back just a little?"*

**Step 3:** Ask again: *"How do I feel toward this part now?"*

______________________________________________________________________________

**Step 4:** Keep asking the judging part to step back until you feel even a hint of curiosity or compassion. That's Self.

The feeling of Self is: ____________________________________________________________

*Practice this toggle throughout the week: Part → Ask to step back → Self*

## Building a Relationship With Your Inner Family

You've met your protectors, sensed your exiles, and accessed Self. Now you learn to relate to them instead of controlling them.

This might feel strange at first. You're used to being caught in internal negotiation (trying to shut down the anxious part, override the critical part, numb the sad part). The idea of having a conversation with these parts, treating them like real beings with valid concerns, probably sounds odd.

But that's exactly what they need. Parts don't transform because you fight them. They transform because you witness them with compassion. When a part feels heard by Self (really heard, really seen) it begins to relax. It doesn't have to be so extreme anymore. It can trust you to lead.

You can do this through journaling, visualization, or simple inner dialogue. What matters is approaching parts with curiosity and compassion, not an agenda to change them.

Use the 6 F sequence as a gentle map, not a script:

Find the part, Focus on it, Flesh it out, Feel toward it, beFriend it, and ask its Fear.

That last question ("What are you afraid would happen?") is the key. Every part has a fear driving its behavior. The perfectionist is afraid you'll be rejected if you're not flawless. The numb part is afraid you'll be destroyed by feeling. The people-pleaser is afraid you'll be abandoned if you say no. When you understand the fear, you understand the part.

Check in briefly each day. Consistency builds trust.

When you start this practice, parts might test you. Parts test reliability the way any hurt being would. They need proof over time. They might get louder, more demanding, more extreme. They're checking: "Are you really going to stay? Or will you abandon me like everyone else?" Don't take the bait. Don't fight back. Just keep showing up. Keep listening. Keep responding with compassion.

Over time, parts begin to trust. The critic softens. The anxious part calms. The numb part allows feeling. They don't disappear (they're still there) but they're no longer running the show. They've handed leadership over to Self.

That's self-leadership: when Self is leading, parts can relax into their natural, non-extreme roles. The critic becomes discernment. The protector becomes healthy caution. The vulnerable part becomes openness. They do what they were designed to do without the desperation trauma created.

Parts learn safety through repetition, not intensity. When you keep showing up, your inner world becomes a family again.

---

## ✏ EXERCISE: First Parts Dialogue

---

Choose one part to dialogue with (anxious part, inner critic, people-pleaser, angry part).

The part I'm dialoging with: ______________________________________________________________

**Step 1:** Get into Self (calm, curious, compassionate). Ask the part: *"What do you want me to know?"*

Let the part answer without censoring:

______________________________________________________________________________

______________________________________________________________________________

______________________________________________________________________________

**Step 2:** Respond from Self with curiosity and compassion:

______________________________________________________________________________

______________________________________________________________________________

______________________________________________________________________________

**Step 3:** Ask: *"What are you afraid will happen if you don't do this job?"*

The part's fear:

______________________________________________________________________________

______________________________________________________________________________

______________________________________________________________________________

**Step 4:** Let the part know you'll check in again. Parts need to know this isn't one-time.

What I want this part to know:

______________________________________________________________________________

______________________________________________________________________________

______________________________________________________________________________

Use this template anytime you need to dialogue with a part.

# Chapter 9:
# Stop Anxiety Attacks Before They Take Over

*"Anxiety is the dizziness of freedom." — Søren Kierkegaard*

Your chest tightens. Your breath becomes shallow. Your heart races like you're being chased, but you're just sitting at your desk. Your mind screams danger while your eyes see safety. Within seconds, you're spiraling, convinced you're dying, losing your mind, or about to collapse.

You've learned how your nervous system responds to threat. Now you'll learn how to stop anxiety before it peaks, using the same awareness and body tools in real time.

The opportunity lies in those first seconds when the alarm starts building. Your body sends warning signals long before panic surges. A flutter in your stomach. A shift in your breathing. A particular thought that starts the spiral. These signals are your early warning system, and learning to read them changes everything.

This chapter teaches you to catch the wave before it crashes. You'll learn to identify your personal alarm signature, interrupt the cascade in its early stages, and build practical tools that work when you need them most. The body's whisper always comes first. Learning to notice it is where real control begins.

## Reading the Early Warning Signs Your Body Sends

Anxiety doesn't ambush you. It builds.

Most people experience panic as sudden and overwhelming, appearing out of nowhere. But if you could rewind the moments before a surge, you'd find clues. A subtle tightness in your throat. Your hands getting colder. Your thoughts speeding up just slightly.

Your nervous system signals activation through changes in breath, temperature, and muscle tone. Recognizing them early gives you choice.

Think of anxiety as having distinct phases. First comes the whisper: those initial physical changes that signal your system is shifting toward activation. Then comes the build: sensations intensify, thoughts accelerate, your body prepares for threat. Finally comes the peak: full alarm, where symptoms feel overwhelming and control seems impossible.

Here's the crucial part: intervention during the whisper phase is exponentially more effective than intervention at the peak. When you catch anxiety in its first 30 to 60 seconds, you're working with a system that's just beginning to activate. You can guide it back toward regulation with minimal effort.

Your anxiety has a signature. Every person's system activates differently. Some people feel it first in their chest, with tightness or pressure that gradually builds. Others notice it in their stomach, a sensation of dropping or churning. Your hands might tingle. Your vision might narrow. Your jaw might clench.

Pay attention to where your body speaks first. That location is your early warning system. One woman discovered her alarm always began with a specific sensation in her throat, as if something were stuck there. Once she recognized this pattern, she had a 60-second window to intervene. A man realized his first sign was always his left shoulder tensing, pulling up toward his ear.

Common early cues include: Change in breath rhythm, shift in body temperature, tightening jaw or shoulders, racing or scattered thoughts, sudden urge to escape or check phone.

The earliest signs often include subtle changes you might dismiss. Your system is preparing for action before you consciously register threat.

Awareness grows through review, not constant monitoring. You're not trying to watch every sensation, waiting anxiously for anxiety to appear. You're simply building awareness of how your particular system expresses stress. This awareness comes from reflection after an episode, not hypervigilance during calm.

What you're learning is pattern recognition. The more you understand how your alarm builds, the more opportunities you have to intervene early. Each time you successfully catch the whisper, your confidence grows. Pause. Notice where your body speaks first.

---

### ✏ EXERCISE: My Anxiety Early Warning System

---

Think back to your three most recent anxiety episodes. For each one, identify the earliest sign you can remember before it became overwhelming.

**Episode 1**

First physical sensation: ______________________________________________________________

First thought: ______________________________________________________________________

Time from first sign to peak: _______________________________________________________

**Episode 2**

First physical sensation: ______________________________________________________________

First thought: ______________________________________________________________________

Time from first sign to peak: _______________________________________________________

**Episode 3**

First physical sensation: ____________________________________________

First thought: ____________________________________________

Time from first sign to peak: ____________________________________________

**My Patterns**

My alarm typically starts with: ____________________________________________

My earliest warning sign is: ____________________________________________

My window for intervention is approximately: ____________________________________________

Keep this page as reference for early intervention.

## Breathing Techniques That Calm Your Nervous System Fast

Your breath is a direct line to your system, but not in the way you've probably been told.

The standard advice during panic is "take a deep breath," but this often backfires. Deep inhales can add activation when you're already flooded. What calms your system is the opposite: a long, slow exhale.

Long exhalation signals safety to the body. Your heart rate slows. Your blood pressure decreases. Your system receives the message that threat is passing.

### Extended Exhale (4 in, 6-8 out)

Breathe in through your nose for four counts. Pause briefly. Exhale through your mouth or nose for six to eight counts, letting the breath empty completely. You're not trying to fill your lungs to capacity. You're breathing fully, allowing your diaphragm to move, but without strain. The focus is on the rhythm: shorter inhale, longer exhale.

*Notice what changes in your chest or shoulders after each round.*

### Box Breathing (4-4-4-4)

Breathe in for four counts. Hold for four counts. Exhale for four counts. Hold empty for four counts. The counting and holding occupy your attention, interrupting mental loops while your system recalibrates.

*Let your jaw soften as you practice.*

### Physiological Sigh (inhale-inhale-long exhale)

Breathe in through your nose, then before exhaling, take a second quick inhale on top of the first. Release a long, slow exhale through your mouth. One or two physiological sighs can shift your state quickly.

*Feel the release in your upper back.*

Not everyone can use breath as an anchor. For some, focusing on breath increases activation rather than decreasing it. If you notice breathwork making things worse, try these modifications: keep your eyes open instead of closed, breathe while moving (walking, swaying, rocking), or place your hand on your chest or belly to add a touch anchor alongside the breath.

If breath focus feels impossible, movement becomes your primary tool.

The key with any breathing technique is practice during calm, not just deployment during crisis. Your system learns patterns through repetition. Practice these techniques when you're regulated, building the pathway so it's available when you need it.

Different techniques work for different phases. Extended exhale breathing works well for early intervention. Box breathing is effective for moderate activation, when you need structure and focus. The physiological sigh works for acute moments, quickly shifting your state when the alarm spikes suddenly.

---

**EXERCISE: Three Breathing Tools Practice**

---

Try each breathing technique for one minute while calm. Notice which one feels most accessible to you.

**Extended Exhale:** Inhale for 4 counts, exhale for 7 counts (1 minute)

How this felt: ______________________________________________________________________

**Box Breathing:** Inhale 4, hold 4, exhale 4, hold 4 (1 minute)

How this felt: ______________________________________________________________________

**Physiological Sigh:** Inhale-inhale-long exhale (1 minute)

How this felt: ______________________________________________________________________

**My Toolkit:** Most natural technique: ______________________________________________________

I'll use for early alarm: ____________________________________________________________

I'll use for peak activation: _________________________________________________________

Practice your chosen techniques daily this week, even when calm.

## Moving Your Body to Discharge Panic Energy

Your body prepares for action long before your mind catches up.

When activation builds, give it movement within your capacity range. Movement lets activation complete without overwhelming you.

**Full-Body Movements (in private)**

Stand with your knees slightly bent and begin shaking your hands, then your arms, then your whole body. Let the movement be loose and uncontrolled. Shake for 30 to 60 seconds, then pause and notice how you feel.

Jump in place, bounce on your toes, or do jumping jacks. A minute of jumping can shift your state, signaling your system that action has been taken.

Stand facing a wall and push against it with your hands and arms, engaging your chest and shoulder muscles. Push firmly for 10 to 15 seconds, then release.

**Subtle Movements (in public)**

Take a brisk walk, letting your arms swing naturally. The bilateral rhythm of walking (left foot, right foot, alternating sides) helps regulate your system.

Clench your fists for a few seconds, then release. Roll your shoulders back several times. These smaller movements still create discharge.

**Seated Movements (at work or when restricted)**

Press your feet firmly into the floor as if you're pushing through it. Tap your feet under your desk. Do alternating knee taps with opposite hands. Tense and release your leg muscles.

The goal isn't to eliminate all physical sensation. The goal is to prevent the building pressure from reaching overwhelm. Movement creates a release valve, lowering intensity from unbearable to manageable.

Create your own movement menu. Know what you can do in private when you have space. Know what you can do in public when you need subtlety. Know what you can do at work, in your car, or anywhere else the alarm might appear. Having options prepared means you don't have to think during crisis. Let your body find its own rhythm.

---

### ✏ EXERCISE: Anxiety Discharge Movement Menu

---

Create your personal menu of movements for different settings. Try each at least once while calm.

**In Private:**

- Shake whole body ☐
- Jump in place ☐
- Push against wall ☐

Most effective: ________________________________________________________________

**In Public:**

- Brisk walk ☐
- Clench/release fists ☐
- Shoulder rolls ☐

Most discrete: ______________________________________________________________________________

**At Work/Seated:**

- Press feet into floor ☐
- Tap feet ☐
- Alternating knee taps ☐

Most helpful: ______________________________________________________________________________

Practice these movements so they're automatic when activation hits.

## Creating a Personalized Anxiety Interrupt Plan

The middle of a panic surge is not the time to figure out what to do.

When your system is flooded, your planning center goes offline. You can't think clearly. You can't weigh options. This is why you need a plan created in advance. Decide your sequence before the alarm starts.

Think of this as an "if-then" protocol. If I notice these specific early warning signs, then I do this specific action. Clear, concrete steps work under stress. Vague intentions don't.

Your plan should include multiple tools because what works today might not work tomorrow. Sometimes breathing is accessible. Sometimes movement is what you need. Having backup options means you're never stuck relying on a single technique.

Start with your early warning signs from the first exercise. What signals tell you the alarm is beginning? Those signals are your "if" statement.

Your first response should be your most effective early intervention tool. For most people, this is either a breathing technique or a subtle movement. Choose whichever one you know works best for catching activation in its first stage. This is your go-to, the action you take within 60 seconds of noticing the early signs.

If your first response doesn't shift your state within a minute or two, you need a backup plan. Maybe you started with extended exhale breathing but you're still feeling activated. Your backup might be to add movement. Or maybe you started with movement but you need more. Your backup might be box breathing to give your mind structure.

Include options for different contexts. What if you're in a meeting and can't leave? What if you're driving? What if you're in bed trying to sleep? Having subtle, seated options alongside more active ones means you can always do something.

Use sensory grounding to orient to the present moment when catastrophic thoughts take over. This cognitive intervention works best after you've done some physical regulation first. Step one is physical: shift your breath or move your body. Step two is mental: ground or re-orient.

After the wave passes, you need a completion step. What will you do to close the experience rather than just moving on? This might be a few minutes of gentle movement, some journaling, or simply sitting quietly and noticing that you survived.

Include support in your plan. Who can you reach out to if you need connection? This isn't about having someone rescue you. It's about knowing you have someone you can text or call if you need another human's presence.

Practice your plan mentally. Visualization creates pathways just like physical practice does. Rehearse this sequence several times a week. When real activation appears, your system will recognize the pattern and follow it more easily.

Post your plan somewhere visible. Your bathroom mirror, your phone's home screen, a note in your wallet. You won't have to try to recall your plan in the moment. You can simply read it and follow it.

Consistency builds trust in your own system, just as it did with your inner work. The preparation itself reduces the alarm's power.

---

### ✏ EXERCISE: My Anxiety Interrupt Protocol

---

**EXERCISE:**

Create your personalized plan using tools from this chapter. Write it clearly so you can reference it during activation.

Early signs I'll watch for:

__________________________________________________

First response (within 60 seconds):

__________________________________________________

If that doesn't work, next I'll try:

__________________________________________________

If I'm in public/can't leave:

__________________________________________________

After the wave passes:

---

Support person I can reach out to:

---

Where I'll post this plan:

---

*Mentally rehearse this plan three times this week.*

## Rewiring Your Response to Triggers Over Time

Managing the alarm today is different from healing it for the long term.

The tools in this chapter help you interrupt panic surges in the moment, preventing escalation and building confidence. These are essential skills, but they're not the endpoint. Acute intervention keeps you safe now. Rewiring your system creates lasting change.

Right now, your system has learned that certain situations are dangerous. Maybe crowded spaces trigger the alarm. Maybe driving on highways does. Maybe conflict or uncertainty does. These triggers aren't random. They're rooted in past experiences, times when your system registered threat and created a protective pattern. Healing means teaching your system something new. You need to create new experiences, moments when you encounter the trigger and survive without catastrophe. Repeated experiences of "I was okay" gradually recalibrate the threat detection system.

This happens through gradual exposure combined with somatic support. You're not forcing yourself into overwhelming situations, hoping to power through. You're taking small steps that challenge your system without flooding it. Stay within the range where you can still think and breathe clearly. When you're outside that range (over-activated or under-activated), your system is in survival mode and learning is impossible. The goal of gradual exposure is staying inside your capacity range while slowly expanding it.

**Steps for gradual expansion:**

- **Choose one trigger.** Pick something you've been avoiding that impacts your life.
- **Take the smallest step within your capacity range.** If you're avoiding crowded places, the smallest step might be standing outside a busy store for two minutes, not even going in. The step should feel manageable, maybe even slightly boring.
- **Use breath or movement to stay present.** This is where everything from previous chapters comes together. These tools keep you in your range while you're approaching the trigger.
- **Notice: Did I survive? Am I okay?** This conscious acknowledgment matters. Your system needs to register that the feared outcome didn't happen.

- **Repeat until it feels neutral.** Your system learns through repetition, not through single heroic efforts. Three successful experiences of standing outside the store teaches your system more than one experience of forcing yourself through the entire trip while dissociated.

You'll know you're ready for the next step when the current one feels genuinely boring or neutral. Not easy necessarily, but not activating anymore. That's your signal to increase difficulty slightly. Setbacks will happen. You'll have days when a step that felt manageable last week suddenly feels impossible. Your capacity range fluctuates based on sleep, stress, overall nervous system state. On hard days, go back to an earlier step that still feels doable. This is working with your current capacity rather than against it. The timeline for this work is gradual. You're not trying to eliminate anxiety in a month. You're building capacity over time, allowing your system to integrate new information at its own pace. Some people move through their steps quickly. Others need months at each stage. Both are normal.

You're not just trying to tolerate triggers without panicking. You're trying to expand your life, reclaiming activities and situations the alarm has taken from you. Each step toward a trigger is a step toward freedom. Each small success teaches your system that safety can return faster than fear.

---

### EXERCISE: Anxiety Tolerance Building Plan

---

Create a gradual exposure plan for one trigger, using somatic tools to support your system.

Trigger I want to work with:________________________________________________________________

Why I avoid it:_____________________________________________________________________________

Smallest possible step:___________________________________________________________________

Next 3-4 steps in my hierarchy:

1. ________________________________________________________________________________
2. ________________________________________________________________________________
3. ________________________________________________________________________________
4. ________________________________________________________________________________

Somatic tools I'll use:

________________________________________________________________________________________

How I'll know I'm ready for the next step:______________________________________________

Timeline: Start date: __________________ I'll repeat each step ______ times before moving to the next.

Review your progress weekly and adjust as needed.

# Chapter 10:
# Healing Depression Through the Body

*"The opposite of depression is not happiness, but vitality." — Andrew Solomon*

It's a heaviness so profound that even breathing feels like work. Getting out of bed is heroic. Showering is exhausting. You're enduring, not living. This is depression, and it doesn't just live in your thoughts. It lives in your bones. Your limbs feel weighted down. Your chest is compressed. Even movement feels impossible. People tell you to "think positive" or "just push through," but they don't understand: this isn't about willpower. Your system has entered deep conservation mode. Depression isn't an emotion. It's a state your body enters when it no longer expects safety. Earlier, you learned how the nervous system responds to threat through activation. Depression is the opposite state: the body's energy collapses inward. Your system hasn't failed. It's protecting you through immobility. When threat felt inescapable for too long, your body learned to shut down everything nonessential. Sensation, motivation, joy. The volume turned down on life itself.

Traditional approaches to depression often focus exclusively on thoughts and emotions. But if you've been depressed for any length of time, you already know: you can't think your way out of this. Your body is stuck in a state of profound shutdown, and until you address that shutdown at the physiological level, the heaviness persists. Because depression is embodied, body-based interventions can reach it in ways that thoughts alone cannot. This chapter isn't about forcing yourself to exercise or pretending to feel grateful when you can't feel anything at all. It's about micro-movements. Tiny sparks of aliveness. Working with, not against, a body that has gone into hibernation mode. You can begin exactly where you are, with what's available. This chapter shows how to rekindle movement and contact from that frozen place. It meets you in the depths and offers small, doable pathways back to vitality.

## Why Depression Feels Like Living in a Frozen Body

Your system protects you through stillness. Your energy has slowed to survive. When your nervous system perceives threat it cannot escape, it has options: fight, flee, or shut down. Shutdown is what happens when fighting won't work and running isn't possible. Your system turns off all nonessential functions to conserve energy and wait out the danger. In moments of acute overwhelm, shutdown is adaptive. It helps you survive the unsurvivable. But when that shutdown becomes chronic, when your system never gets the signal that the threat has passed, shutdown becomes depression. This is dorsal vagal collapse. Your body's emergency brake stays on, slowing everything. Your system lowers energy and sensation to keep you safe. Metabolism slows. Movement feels impossible. The world feels distant, muted, unreachable. Depression that emerges from prolonged stress or unresolved trauma is your body stuck in this collapsed state, unable to complete the defensive response it started long ago. Your system is still braced for danger. Your system hasn't yet received the signal that it's safe to return. The shutdown protects you from feeling overwhelming pain. When life hurt too much for too long, your body learned to numb everything. But now, years later, you're not just numb to pain. You're numb to everything. Joy, connection, pleasure, meaning. The protection has become a prison. Pause. Notice what happens in your chest when you read that line. Here's the feedback loop that keeps you stuck: Your body is in shutdown. Because your body is shutdown, your mood is flat and your thoughts are dark. Because your mood is flat and your thoughts are dark, you don't move much. Because you don't move much, your body stays in shutdown. The loop perpetuates itself. The body feels heavy, expressionless, absent from within. Each breath takes effort, as if the air itself weighs something. Your system is doing exactly what it was designed to do in the face of inescapable threat. The problem is simple but profound: the threat has passed. The body hasn't realized it yet.

### EXERCISE: Depression Body Map

This exercise helps you externalize what depression feels like in your body, making the invisible visible and workable. In the space below, draw a simple outline of a human body. Stick figure is fine, no artistic skill required.

Now, using the prompts below, mark your drawing:

- Which parts feel "offline"? (Parts that feel absent, unreachable, or disconnected. Circle or mark with an X.)
- Are there any areas that still feel alive? (Even slightly. Mark these with a star or different color.)
- Reflections: Look at your completed body map. What do you notice? Is the heaviness concentrated in certain areas? Is there more numbness than you expected? Did you find any areas that surprised you?

*Keep this map. You'll reference it as you move through this chapter, and you can create new maps over time to track shifts in how depression lives in your body.*

## Gentle Movement to Thaw Emotional Numbness

When you're depressed, the idea of "exercise" feels impossible. You can barely get out of bed. How are you supposed to go to the gym?

You're not.

This section isn't about exercise. It's about micro-movements. Tiny gestures of aliveness that your system can handle even in its most shutdown state. Movement isn't a demand here. It's an invitation.

Exercise demands energy you don't have. Exploration asks for curiosity you still possess.

Your body has been in hibernation mode. Tiny movements wake it up one cell at a time. Movement isn't release here; it's ignition. When you move, even minimally, you send a signal to your system: *We're still here. We're still alive. Maybe it's safe enough to come online, just a little.*

Start where you are. If you can't get out of bed, stay in bed. If you can sit up, sit up. If you can stand, stand. There's no hierarchy of "good enough" here. Your only job is to find the smallest possible movement and do it with attention.

- Wiggle your fingers or rotate your wrists
- Rock gently side to side
- Stretch your arms overhead while lying down
- Press your feet into the floor or mattress

Choose any movement your body can tolerate, no matter how small.

These aren't exercises. They're experiments. You're testing: What does it feel like to move this part of my body? Does it feel heavy? Tight? Numb? Or does it feel, even slightly, less terrible than staying completely still?

Some movements will feel like pushing through concrete. Others might surprise you with a flicker of relief or release. Some will feel neutral, which, when you're depressed, counts as progress. You're not trying to feel good. You're trying to feel *something.*

This is where moments of aliveness begin. Moments when your system registers even a tiny bit of safety or okayness. A stretch that feels slightly good. A movement that creates a sensation you'd forgotten your body could have. These are the breadcrumbs leading you out of shutdown.

Your depression will tell you that moving is pointless, that it won't help, that you're too tired. That voice is your shutdown state talking. It wants to conserve energy. It wants to stay protected. You don't have to fight it. You just have to do something so small that it can't argue.

Five minutes. That's all. Not because five minutes will cure depression, but because five minutes proves to your system that movement is possible. And possible is the opposite of hopeless.

Each small motion is a quiet act of defiance against numbness.

As the body begins to move again, the next step is reawakening the signals of safety that depression has silenced.

---

### ✎ EXERCISE: Five-Minute Movement Awakening

---

Set a timer for exactly 5 minutes. Not more. This isn't about duration or achievement. It's about gentle exploration.

**What to do:** Find a comfortable position (lying down, sitting, or standing) and experiment with the micro-movements listed below. Move slowly, without force. Your only job is to notice: Does this movement create any sensation at all? Does anything feel slightly different, slightly less numb, or even slightly good?

**Micro-movements to explore:**

- Wiggle your fingers and toes
- Rotate your wrists and ankles slowly
- Rock your body gently side to side
- Stretch your arms overhead (or as far as comfortable)
- Roll your shoulders forward, then backward
- Tilt your head to one side, hold for a breath, then the other side
- Press your feet into the floor or your back into the bed
- Make gentle fists, then release

**Reflection prompts:**

Which movement felt the most accessible (easiest to do)?________________________________________

Did any movement create a sensation you noticed, even if slight or neutral?________________________

Which areas of your body still felt completely offline or numb?___________________________________

On a scale of 1-10, how much resistance did you feel to starting this exercise? ______________________

*Note: You don't need to do this perfectly. You don't even need to do it daily. Whenever you remember, whenever you have five minutes, try again. Each time you move with curiosity instead of force, you're rewiring the pattern.*

## Reawakening Your Safety System

Depression isn't too much activation. It's too much shutdown. This distinction matters because it changes everything about how you approach healing.

When you're anxious, your system is overactive. You need to calm down. But when you're depressed, you're stuck in collapse, and you need to gently come back *up*. Calming techniques that work for anxiety can actually make depression worse by pushing you deeper into shutdown.

What you need is gentle activation of your safety system. The capacity to be present, to engage, to feel like you're part of the world again. This isn't manic energy or forced enthusiasm. It's the quiet possibility of connection.

Gentle sound, touch, and breath cues remind your system that connection is safe again.

Humming stimulates your system through vibration in your throat and chest. When you hum, you create a physical sensation that your body can't ignore. The vibration travels through pathways that signal safety, reminding your system that you're alive, that your body can generate sensation, that you have a voice.

Cold water on your face creates a brief reset. When cold water touches your face, your system shifts almost instantly. Your heart rate adjusts in a controlled way, and your body prioritizes essential functions. This creates a moment of clarity, pulling you out of shutdown and into a more regulated state.

Hum softly, splash cool water on your face, or sit near someone safe. These are small ways of saying to your body: we survived.

Pause. Notice if your breath or posture changes, even slightly.

Social connection, even brief and minimal, is one of the most powerful ways to shift out of shutdown. Your system learns safety through presence. You don't need to talk about your pain. Just let another heartbeat exist near yours. Sometimes it means texting a friend. Sometimes it means sitting near another person. Sometimes it means petting your dog.

Depression tells you to isolate. It tells you that you're a burden, that nobody wants to hear from you, that you should stay alone until you feel better. This is shutdown talking. Isolation perpetuates shutdown. Connection, even minimal connection, offers your system a different possibility.

Small pleasures also activate your safety system. A warm drink. Soft fabric. Sunlight on your skin. These aren't indulgences; they're medicine. When your body registers something pleasant, even for a moment, it shifts slightly out of shutdown and toward safety. You're teaching your system that the world can offer something other than threat or numbness.

You're not trying to force happiness. You're not trying to "snap out of it." You're gently coaxing a hibernating animal awake. You're offering your body tiny signals of safety and waiting to see what happens.

Connection, sound, and gentle cold are bridges back to life.

---

## EXERCISE: Safety Signal Practice

---

This week, you'll try three different practices that gently activate your safety system. Your goal isn't to do all of them every day. It's to discover which one feels most accessible to you right now.

Try each practice once, then choose your anchor practice for the week.

**Hum** Sit or lie comfortably. Take a breath in, and as you exhale, hum a simple tone. It doesn't need to be a tune, just a steady hum for the length of your exhale. Do this for 1 minute.

How did this feel? ____________________________________________________________

**Cold Water** Splash cold water on your face, or hold a cold, damp cloth against your forehead and cheeks for 30 seconds. Alternatively, hold an ice cube in your hand and pay attention to the sensation.

How did this feel? ____________________________________________________________

**Brief Connection** Send a text to one person, sit near someone (even without talking), or spend a few minutes with a pet. Let yourself be in the presence of another living being without any agenda.

How did this feel? ____________________________________________________________

**Choose your anchor practice:** Which one felt least effortful? Which one could you imagine doing even on your worst day?

My anchor practice for this week is: ____________________________________________

**Commitment:** I will do my anchor practice once daily for seven days.

Days completed: ☐ Day 1 ☐ Day 2 ☐ Day 3 ☐ Day 4 ☐ Day 5 ☐ Day 6 ☐ Day 7

**Reflection after one week:** What did you notice about your body or mood after practicing this regularly?

______________________________________________________________________________

______________________________________________________________________________

______________________________________________________________________________

## Finding Tiny Sparks of Aliveness Again

Depression is a liar. It tells you that nothing feels good, that nothing will ever feel good again, that you're permanently broken. But depression lies not by creating feelings, but by removing your ability to notice the ones that still exist.

Moments of less heaviness are signs of life returning.

These moments are still there. You've just lost the capacity to see them. The warmth of the sun on your skin. The taste of coffee. The weight of your pet curled against you. The sound of rain. The softness of your pillow. These aren't big feelings. They're flickers. But flickers are enough.

The practice of finding these moments isn't about forcing gratitude or pretending you feel better than you do. It's about training your attention to notice when something registers as even slightly less awful. You're teaching your brain that aliveness still exists, even if only in fragments.

Attention rewires your brain; noticing aliveness makes more of it.

Depression will resist this. It will tell you that noticing small good things is pointless, naive, or insulting to your pain. It will tell you that you don't deserve to feel good. It will tell you that if you let yourself feel even a flicker of pleasure, it will be ripped away and you'll be crushed again.

These are protective thoughts from a system that's trying to keep you safe by keeping you numb. You don't have to fight them. You just have to gently persist in noticing what's actually happening in your sensory experience, not what your thoughts say about it.

Touch, taste, listen, and look without judging. Let sensation be the first language your body relearns.

Touch something soft. A blanket, a pet, your own hair. What does softness actually feel like? Not what you think about it, but the sensation itself.

Taste something you don't hate. Can you notice the flavor for five seconds without judging yourself for it?

Listen to a sound that doesn't make things worse. Rain. Music. Birds. Can you let your attention rest on the sound instead of on your thoughts?

Look at something that doesn't add to the heaviness. A tree outside your window. A color you don't hate. Can you look at it for ten seconds without turning away?

The practice is simple: when something feels even slightly less heavy, you linger there. You don't rush past it. You don't dismiss it. You let your system register that this moment is different from the numbness. Even if it only lasts five seconds, those five seconds matter.

You might feel guilty when something feels good. You might think, "I don't deserve this," or "This won't last, so why bother noticing?" These thoughts are common, and they're part of depression's protective mechanism. You can acknowledge them without letting them erase the flicker.

Building capacity for positive sensation happens gradually. You can't go from complete shutdown to joy in one leap. But you can go from shutdown to neutral. From neutral to slightly okay. From slightly okay to a brief flicker of something pleasant. These micro-shifts accumulate.

Your system learns through repetition. Each flicker reminds your body that life is still here.

Your job this week isn't to feel happy. It's to notice one moment per day when your system registered something other than heavy or numb.

Five seconds of noticing is enough. Five seconds is life entering again.

---

### EXERCISE: Daily Aliveness Log

---

For the next seven days, you'll practice noticing one small moment of aliveness each day. These aren't big experiences. They're tiny flickers that you might normally overlook.

**Instructions:** Each day, pay attention to moments when something feels even slightly less heavy. It might be a sensory experience, a brief interaction, or a moment when your body felt fractionally different. Write it down using the prompt below.

**Day 1** Today I noticed: ______________________________________________

**Day 2** Today I noticed: ______________________________________________

**Day 3** Today I noticed: ______________________________________________

**Day 4** Today I noticed: ______________________________________________

**Day 5** Today I noticed: ______________________________________________

**Day 6** Today I noticed: ______________________________________________

**Day 7** Today I noticed: ______________________________________________

**Reflection:** Look back at your seven moments. Did you notice any patterns? Were certain types of experiences easier to notice than others? Did the practice of looking for moments of aliveness change anything about your daily experience?

______________________________________________________________________

______________________________________________________________________

______________________________________________________________________

*Note: Keep this practice going beyond the seven days if it feels helpful. Some people find that the daily aliveness log becomes a grounding ritual that subtly shifts their relationship with depression over time.*

## Building Momentum Without Overwhelming Yourself

There's a paradox at the heart of depression recovery: you'll feel better when you do things, but depression makes it feel impossible to do things. Waiting until you "feel like it" keeps you stuck indefinitely.

Action precedes feeling. Even small actions start the climb.

This is called behavioral activation, and it's one of the most evidence-based approaches to depression. But the version that works for trauma-based depression is different. It's not about productivity or achievement. It's about tiny commitments that you can keep even on your worst days. It's about celebrating micro-victories as victories, not dismissing them as "not enough."

Your depression will tell you that brushing your teeth doesn't count. That opening the blinds doesn't matter. That texting one friend is trivial. But these actions send a signal to your system: *I made a commitment to myself, and I kept it.* That signal, repeated over time, begins to shift the feedback loop.

Small actions create small shifts. Small shifts create slightly more capacity. Slightly more capacity allows for slightly bigger actions. This isn't linear. You'll have days where nothing feels possible, and that's part of the process. But over time, the momentum builds.

Depression waits. Healing moves, even slightly.

You get dressed, and then your mood shifts slightly. You step outside for 60 seconds, and then your body registers that the world still exists. You drink a glass of water, and then your system has fractionally more capacity. The action comes first.

This doesn't mean white-knuckling through tasks you hate. It means choosing one commitment so small that resistance can't stop you. One thing you can do even when everything feels impossible. That becomes your anchor.

Open blinds. Brush teeth. Drink water. Text one person. Each counts.

Celebrating micro-victories is essential. When you brush your teeth, you acknowledge it. When you open the blinds, you notice it. When you text one person, you recognize that you did something your depression told you was impossible. This isn't toxic positivity. It's accurate acknowledgment of what's true. You did something. That matters.

Notice how your shoulders respond when you acknowledge effort instead of failure.

Self-compassion is the foundation here, not self-discipline. Harsh self-criticism keeps your system in shutdown. When you berate yourself for not doing more, for not being better, for still being depressed, you reinforce the state you're trying to move out of. But when you speak to yourself with the same kindness you'd offer a friend in pain, something shifts.

Some days the weight returns. That's information, not failure.

On those days, you track what happened without judgment. You notice, "Today I didn't do the thing." And then, when you can, you do it again.

The practice isn't about perfection. It's about building the pathway of "I make small commitments to myself, and I keep them when I can." Over time, that pathway strengthens. Your capacity grows. The momentum builds, slowly but steadily.

Small commitments restore trust between you and your body.

---

### EXERCISE: One Commitment Builder

---

This exercise helps you identify a single, sustainable action that you can commit to even on your worst days. The goal isn't to achieve more. It's to build the practice of making and keeping commitments to yourself.

**Step 1: Identify your one commitment**

Choose ONE action from the list below, or create your own. It must be so small that you can do it even when depression is at its worst.

Possible commitments:

- Brush teeth once per day
- Open blinds or curtains in the morning
- Drink one full glass of water
- Step outside for 60 seconds
- Text or message one person
- Make your bed
- Wash your face
- Eat one meal sitting down
- Take your medication (if applicable)
- Other: ____________________________________________

My one commitment for this week is: ____________________________________________

**Step 2: Track your commitment**

For seven days, track whether you completed your commitment. If you did it, check the box. If you didn't, leave it blank. No judgment either way. Just data.

☐ Day 1 ☐ Day 2 ☐ Day 3 ☐ Day 4 ☐ Day 5 ☐ Day 6 ☐ Day 7

**Step 3: Reflect without judgment**

After seven days, review your tracking.

How many days did you complete your commitment? _______

On days you completed it, what did you notice about your mood or energy afterward?

___________________________________________________________________________

___________________________________________________________________________

___________________________________________________________________________

On days you didn't complete it, what got in the way?

___________________________________________________________________________

___________________________________________________________________________

___________________________________________________________________________

What did you learn about yourself from this practice?

___________________________________________________________________________

___________________________________________________________________________

___________________________________________________________________________

**Step 4: Continue or adjust**

Do you want to continue with the same commitment for another week, or adjust to something different?

☐ Continue with the same commitment

☐ Adjust to a new commitment: ______________________________________________

___________________________________________________________________________

*Note: Consistency, not perfection, rebuilds vitality. Each small act reminds your body that life is returning.*

# Chapter 11: Somatic Practices for Everyday Regulation

*"How we spend our days is, of course, how we spend our lives." — Annie Dillard*

This chapter is about maintenance, the everyday regulation that keeps healing alive once the crisis has passed.

You've learned to feel what's happening in your body. You've built safety, released trapped emotions, worked with your parts, processed pain. These are the breakthroughs that matter. But here's what nobody mentions in those transformative therapy moments: healing doesn't live in the breakthrough. It lives in what you do Tuesday morning when you're tired, or Thursday afternoon when work gets overwhelming, or Sunday night when anxiety about the week ahead starts climbing your spine.

Healing is a practice, not an event.

The real work happens in how you breathe when your alarm goes off, how you transition from one task to another, how you help your nervous system settle before sleep. It happens in the space between crisis and calm, in the ordinary moments that make up most of your life. This chapter isn't about what to do when everything falls apart. It's about nervous system hygiene—the ordinary care that prevents collapse before it begins.

These aren't new methods. They're the same principles you've already practiced, integrated into the rhythm of daily life.

Your system thrives on small, steady attention. Daily tending matters more than occasional intensity. This isn't about adding complicated self-care patterns to an already overwhelming life. You don't need another hour-long morning sequence or ten-step evening process. You need simple, sustainable practices woven into the structure of days you're already living. You need tools that take ninety seconds, that work in public spaces, that function when you're exhausted or rushed or barely holding it together.

The practices in this chapter are meant to become invisible infrastructure. They're the foundation that makes everything else possible, the maintenance that prevents the need for emergency repair. Small, consistent, sustainable. That's how real healing happens.

## Morning Practices to Start Your Day Grounded

Your nervous system wakes up open and impressionable. In the first hour after opening your eyes, you set the baseline for the entire day ahead. This isn't mystical or metaphorical. It's neuroscience. The tone you establish in those early minutes, your nervous system carries it forward.

Most people reach for their phone before their feet touch the floor. They scroll through emails, news, messages, letting the world's demands flood their system before they've even said hello to their own body. When you start the day reacting, your system learns urgency instead of safety. They rush through getting ready, skip breakfast or eat it standing up, and arrive at work already activated. By 9 AM, they're running a sympathetic nervous system default, and they wonder why they feel depleted by afternoon.

You're teaching your nervous system that the world is urgent, demanding, and unsafe before you've given it a chance to feel anything else. Starting grounded doesn't require an hour of meditation or elaborate sequences. It requires intentionality. Five minutes of deliberate practice does more than thirty minutes of unconscious rushing. The question isn't "How much time do I have?" but "What do I want my nervous system to know about today?"

Here's what makes a difference: before you touch your phone, before you start mentally listing everything you need to do, you give your body something to anchor to. Maybe that's feeling your feet on the floor. Maybe it's a brief breath or grounding touch with your hand on your chest. Maybe it's stretching in bed for sixty seconds, letting your muscles wake up before your mind takes over.

Pause. Let the morning air touch your skin before the world reaches you.

Then you choose your first sensory experience. Not what's easiest or fastest, but what's intentional. Cold water on your face. Warm tea you actually taste. Natural light instead of blue screen glow. You're not trying to force calm or manufacture peace. You're simply giving your nervous system information that says: you have time, you're safe, you're here. A body check-in comes next. Two minutes, that's all. Notice three sensations before moving on: warmth, tension, or stillness. Tight shoulders? Note it. Butterflies in your stomach? Acknowledge them. Heavy legs? That's information. You're not trying to fix anything yet. You're building the habit of awareness, teaching yourself to notice your body's language first thing, when you still have space to respond before the day's demands take over.

Some people like setting an intention. Not a massive goal or ambitious plan, just one word or phrase for how they want to feel. Steady. Present. Kind to myself. Open. It's a north star, not a requirement. Something to return to when you lose your way. None of this prevents hard days from happening. You'll still face stress, challenges, overwhelm. But you'll face them from a different starting point. Instead of beginning the day already depleted, you begin with a foundation. Instead of reacting from depletion, you respond from ground.

The goal isn't perfection. Some mornings you'll remember, some mornings you'll forget. Some days you'll have fifteen minutes, other days you'll have two. What matters is the pattern you build over time, the relationship you develop with your nervous system in those first waking moments. You're teaching it that you're paying attention, that you care, that you'll show up even in small ways.

This is befriending the morning. Not conquering it or optimizing it, but meeting it with presence. These quiet beginnings shape the rhythm that carries through your day. Pause. Notice how simple attention becomes its own form of care.

### EXERCISE: Design My Morning Anchor

Create a simple morning practice you can sustain (5-15 minutes).

Before touching my phone, I will________________________________________________________

My first intentional sensory experience:____________________________________________

**Body check-in (2 minutes)**

Three sensations I'll notice: _________________________________________________________

My intention word or phrase:_________________________________________________________

**After 7 days, I'll reflect:**

What worked: _____________________________________________________________________

What I'll adjust: __________________________________________________________________

## Midday Check-Ins to Prevent Overwhelm

Stress accumulates quietly. Small pauses prevent overload.

Most of your day probably doesn't allow for long breaks. You can't take thirty-minute walks or hour-long sessions in the middle of work. But you can take ninety seconds. You can excuse yourself to the bathroom and do three minutes of breathing. You can walk to a window. You can roll your shoulders while waiting for your computer to load.

The practice is simple: notice, reset, continue.

**Notice** means checking in with your nervous system state. Not analyzing or explaining it, just naming it. Am I activated right now? Tense? Shut down? Holding my breath? Clenching my jaw? You're gathering data, building the skill of interoceptive awareness throughout the day instead of only at crisis points.

**Reset** means choosing one quick tool to shift your state, even slightly. One long exhale. Shoulder rolls. Standing up and shaking out your arms. Splashing cold water on your wrists. Getting outside for thirty seconds. These aren't elaborate interventions. They're micro-adjustments that remind your nervous system it has options, that you can keep your system within your usable range.

**Continue** means returning to what you were doing, but with a bit more regulation under you. You didn't fix everything. You don't need to. You just prevented the buildup from getting worse. You touched ground.

The resistance to this practice is real. When you're busy, stopping feels counterproductive. When you're stressed, you think you don't have time for breaks. But this is exactly backward. The more pressure you're under, the more you need these check-ins. They're not interruptions to productivity. They're what makes sustained productivity possible.

If you're driving and the car starts veering left, you make a small correction in the moment. You don't wait until you're in the ditch to yank the wheel hard. Your nervous system works the same way. Regular small adjustments prevent the need for major interventions later.

Some days you'll catch yourself early, when activation is mild. Other days you'll catch yourself late, when you're already tipped over. Both are okay. You're building a practice, not executing perfection. The skill develops over time. You'll start noticing stress earlier. You'll recognize your patterns. You'll intervene before crisis becomes your only option.

Set alarms if you need to. Link check-ins to existing habits. Before each meal. After each meeting. Every time you go to the bathroom. Rhythm trains the nervous system better than willpower. Make it automatic so you don't have to remember when you're already depleted.

Your nervous system needs these touchpoints throughout the day. Little reminders that you're paying attention, that you care, that regulation is available.

*Each small correction teaches your system that safety is always within reach.*

---

### ✏ EXERCISE: Midday Regulation Checkpoints

---

Set 3 alarms on your phone during your workday: mid-morning, lunch, and mid-afternoon.

**My check-in times:** ______ AM, ______ PM, ______ PM

**At each alarm, take 60-90 seconds:**

1. **NOTICE:** How's my nervous system? (activated / calm / shut down)
2. **RESET:** One quick tool (circle one you'll try):
    - One long exhale
    - Shoulder rolls
    - Walk to window
    - Cold water on wrists
    - Other: _______________
3. **CONTINUE:** Return to day

**Track for one week:**

Did regular check-ins prevent end-of-day depletion? Yes / No

What I noticed:______________________________________________________________________

## Evening Rituals to Release the Day's Stress

Your body remembers the day until you tell it the day is done.

Every interaction, every deadline, every moment of tension or holding or pushing through gets stored somewhere in your system. You might leave work physically, but your nervous system is still there, replaying conversations, rehearsing tomorrow's worries, carrying the weight of what happened and what might happen next.

Going from high activation straight to bed doesn't work. Your body doesn't have an off switch. It needs a bridge, a transition, a signal that the day is over and it's safe to let go now.

Think about what happens when you don't settle the day's stress before sleep. You lie in bed replaying everything. Your mind won't stop. Your body feels wired and tired at the same time. You finally fall asleep but wake up exhausted because you never actually rested. You carried yesterday's tension into today's baseline, starting each day with a deficit you can't quite name.

Evening practices complete the stress pattern. They help your body finish what the day began so it doesn't follow you into sleep. This isn't about forcing relaxation or manufacturing peace. It's about giving your nervous system permission to shift gears, creating the transition between doing and resting.

Physical release comes first because your body needs to move the energy that's been held all day. This doesn't mean intense exercise. Evening movement helps your body complete what the day began. Stand in your living room and shake out your arms, your legs, your whole body. Roll your shoulders. Do simple yoga stretches. Walk around your house. Dance to one song. You're not trying to exhaust yourself. You're moving stuck energy so it doesn't lodge deeper.

Mental release follows because your mind is still circling. Everything you didn't say, everything you need to remember, everything that's unfinished is taking up space. Write everything circling in your mind. Don't organize—empty. Work stresses, tomorrow's to-do list, conversations you keep replaying, worries about next week. Get it out of your head and onto the page where it can exist without you holding it.

Sensory downregulation helps your body recognize that it's evening now, time to shift. Dim the lights. Put your phone across the room. Make tea or warm milk. Wrap yourself in something soft. You're changing the environment to match the state you want to create. Screens and stimulation keep the body alert long after the day is done. Soft, warm, dim tells it something different.

Gratitude or completion anchors the day in something other than what went wrong. You don't need to manufacture happiness or pretend hard things didn't happen. Just name one thing that went okay. One moment you handled. One person who was kind. One thing your body did for you today. You're training your nervous system to notice what's working alongside what's hard.

Not every night allows for full practices. Sometimes you have fifteen minutes, sometimes you have five. What matters is the consistency of signaling to your body: the day is done, you're safe, you can release now. Even abbreviated versions help. Three minutes of stretching, two minutes of journaling, one minute of breathing. Better than going from full activation to bed with nothing in between.

The resistance here is real. When you're exhausted, the couch and screen feel easier than intentional practice. When you're wired, you want to keep pushing through. But this is exactly when evening practices matter most. They're not one more thing on your list. They're the thing that makes everything else sustainable. When the body releases the day, sleep becomes true rest, not escape. Your morning baseline improves when you're not starting the day already depleted. Your capacity for the next day expands when you've actually rested instead of just lying unconscious for eight hours.

You're teaching your nervous system that days have endings, that stress doesn't have to carry forward, that you know how to close one chapter before opening the next. Your body knows how to let go. You just have to show it the way.

---

### ✎ EXERCISE: Evening Completion Ritual

---

Design a 20-30 minute wind-down practice before bed.

**1. Physical release (5 min):** ____________________________________________

*(Examples: shake body, stretch, gentle yoga, walk, dance to one song)*

**2. Mental release (5 min) - Write everything circling:**

Work: ____________________________________________

Tomorrow: ____________________________________________

Replaying: ____________________________________________

Other: ____________________________________________

**3. Sensory downregulation - I will:**

____________________________________________

*(Examples: dim lights, put phone away, warm tea, soft blanket)*

**4. Completion - One thing that went okay today:**

____________________________________________

**Try for 7 nights. After one week:**

Impact on sleep: ____________________________________________

What worked best: ____________________________________________

## Tracking Your Progress and Celebrating Small Wins

In Chapter 10 you practiced noticing small changes. Tracking brings those changes into focus.

You can't see change when you're inside it. Day to day, healing feels imperceptible. You still have hard moments. You still get triggered. You still struggle. So your brain concludes nothing is working, nothing has changed, you're exactly where you started.

But tracking reveals what memory can't hold. When you write down where you are, what you did, how you felt, patterns emerge over time that you'd never notice in individual moments. You see that three months ago you couldn't identify your emotions at all, and now you can name them most days. You see that panic attacks used to last two hours and now they last twenty minutes. You see that you're using tools before crisis instead of only after.

Tracking isn't judgment. It's witnessing your own process with clarity and care.

The practice is simple: track your baseline, track what you did, track what happened. Not elaborate spreadsheets or complex systems. Just a notebook or phone note where you check in briefly each day. Morning state. Tools used. Challenges faced. Small wins. Evening state.

Some days you'll track good things. Other days everything will feel hard. Both matter. You're not trying to manufacture improvement or force positive thinking. You're gathering honest information about your nervous system, your patterns, your capacity.

What gets noticed can evolve. This isn't a report card where you pass or fail. It's a journal where you learn yourself. Where you notice: I always crash on Thursday afternoons. I regulate better when I move my body in the morning. My nervous system settles faster when I use this tool instead of that one. Weekends require different support than weekdays.

The wins you track don't have to be big. Used a grounding technique when I felt panic rising. That's a win. Asked for what I needed instead of pretending I was fine. Win. Noticed I was in freeze and chose to move anyway. Win. Got out of bed on a hard day. Win. You're training your brain to see capability alongside struggle, to recognize that even small actions matter.

Two weeks of tracking usually reveals clear patterns. Some tools help more than others. Certain situations consistently trigger you. Specific times of day are harder. Sleep quality affects everything. You have more capacity than you thought in some areas, less in others. This information becomes power. You stop guessing what might help and start knowing what does help.

If you used journaling before, this is its daily version—simpler, faster. Reviewing your tracking also lets you celebrate progress that's easy to dismiss. You handled this situation differently than last month. You recovered faster this time. You caught yourself earlier. You tried something new. These shifts feel tiny in the moment but they're evidence that your nervous system is learning, adapting, healing.

Some people resist tracking because it feels like one more task. But tracking takes three minutes a day and saves hours of spinning in "nothing works" thoughts. Some resist because they're afraid to see how bad things are. But tracking shows both the hard and the good, and often reveals you're doing better than depression wants you to believe.

This practice builds self-trust. You're proving to yourself that you notice, that you care, that you show up. You're creating evidence that your nervous system can learn new patterns, that healing is happening even when it doesn't feel dramatic.

Your notes become proof of life—evidence that regulation is taking root.

*Each entry is a conversation with yourself, a record of showing up.*

---

### ✏ EXERCISE: My Nervous System Tracking Journal

---

Use this page as your daily template for 2 weeks. Copy this format into a notebook or phone note app, and fill it out each day.

**Morning baseline:** (1-10 or word) ____________________________________________________________

Tools I used today:____________________________________________________________

Challenges faced:____________________________________________________________

Wins (even tiny):____________________________________________________________

**Evening state:** (1-10 or word) ____________________________________________________________

**After 2 weeks, review and answer:**

**Patterns I notice:**

Times/situations that are hardest: ____________________________________________________

Tools that help most: ____________________________________________________________

**Progress I can see:**

What I'm doing differently: ____________________________________________________

What I can celebrate: ____________________________________________________________

**Adjustments to make:**

______________________________________________________________________________

______________________________________________________________________________

## Building a Sustainable Healing Practice

Healing isn't a destination you reach and then stop. It's a practice you develop, adjust, and return to for the rest of your life. This reality disappoints people who want to "finish" healing, who want to arrive at some future state where they never struggle again. But that's not how nervous systems work. That's not how life works.

You don't heal once and stay healed. You practice regulation, you build capacity, you develop relationship with your body and nervous system that sustains you through whatever comes next. Some seasons require intensive support. Other seasons need only maintenance. The practice flexes with life, but it never stops entirely.

This is what makes healing sustainable: accepting that you're building a practice, not completing a project.

Most people approach healing with intensity. They throw themselves into every tool, every technique, every recommendation they encounter. They do all the things perfectly for three weeks, then burn out and do nothing for three months. The all-or-nothing approach guarantees failure because it's not sustainable. You can't maintain that level of intensity long-term. Nobody can.

Sustainability means doing less more consistently rather than doing everything briefly. It means having practices you return to, not practices you execute perfectly every single day. It means building flex into your system so you don't collapse when life gets hard.

Think in layers, not levels of success.

You have three tiers of practice. **Tier 1** is your non-negotiables, the absolute basics you do even on your worst days. Maybe that's just a brief breath or grounding touch in the morning and acknowledging one feeling before bed. That's it. Tier 1 keeps you afloat.

**Tier 2** is your regular practice, what you do most days when life is normal. Morning grounding, midday check-ins, evening pattern, some body awareness throughout the day. Tier 2 keeps you steady.

**Tier 3** is deeper healing work, what you do when you have extra capacity and resources. Longer practices, more intensive processing, exploring new tools, working with a therapist on bigger issues. Tier 3 deepens the work when you have capacity.

The flexibility matters. When life gets overwhelming, you drop to Tier 1 without guilt or shame. You're not failing. You're adapting. When things stabilize, you return to Tier 2. When you have capacity, you expand to Tier 3. The practice moves with you instead of demanding you maintain the same level regardless of circumstances.

This approach removes the binary thinking that sabotages most healing attempts. You're not "on track" or "failing." You're practicing at whatever level your current life allows, trusting that the practice itself is what matters, not perfect execution.

Returning after falling off is part of the practice. You will forget. You will get busy or overwhelmed or depressed and stop doing anything for days or weeks. This doesn't erase your progress. It doesn't mean you have to start over. You just return. Pick up where you left off. Start again with Tier 1 if that's all you can manage. Each return strengthens trust between you and your system. The practice is always there waiting, never judging, ready whenever you come back. Building a sustainable practice means making peace with imperfection. You won't do everything right. You won't remember every tool. Some days will feel like regression. But over time, the overall trajectory moves toward more regulation, more capacity, more healing. Not linear progress, but real progress nonetheless.

You're not trying to become someone who never struggles. You're becoming someone who knows how to work with struggle, who has tools to reach for, who trusts their nervous system can shift even when it feels impossible. You're building a relationship with your body that says: I'm here, I'm paying attention, I care what happens to you. That relationship is the healing. Everything else is just practice. You are not finishing healing. You're learning how to live as someone who knows how to come back to safety, again and again. Healing endures not through perfection, but through return—gentle, steady, and alive.

---

### ✎ EXERCISE: My Sustainable Practice Blueprint

---

Create three tiers of practice that flex with your life.

**TIER 1 - Non-negotiables (what I do even on worst days):**

_______________________________________________________________________________

_______________________________________________________________________________

**TIER 2 - Regular practice (what I do most days when life is normal):**

Morning: _______________________________________________________________________

Midday: ________________________________________________________________________

Evening: _______________________________________________________________________

**TIER 3 - Deep healing work (when I have capacity):**

_______________________________________________________________________________

_______________________________________________________________________________

I'm in Tier 1 when: ______________________________________________________________

I'm in Tier 2 when: ______________________________________________________________

I'm in Tier 3 when: ______________________________________________________________

# Chapter 12: Living in a Regulated Body

*"And the day came when the risk to remain tight in a bud was more painful than the risk it took to blossom." — Anaïs Nin*

One morning, you wake up and realize something has shifted. You don't feel like you're bracing against the day. Your body doesn't feel like a battleground. The anxiety is quieter. The weight you once carried feels lighter, as if something inside has begun to breathe again. You're living, not just surviving.

Maybe you notice it when someone raises their voice and you don't freeze. Or when you feel sadness and it moves through you instead of trapping you. Maybe it's simpler: you took a full breath without remembering to. Your shoulders dropped without effort. You laughed and felt it in your chest.

You've done the work of understanding your nervous system, creating steadiness, reconnecting with your body, releasing what's been trapped, and learning to work with your parts. Now comes something different. Taking all that knowledge and letting it dissolve into how you move through the world. Not doing the practices. Being them.

This chapter isn't about maintaining routines. It's about living from what's now innate. Integration. The moment when healing stops being something separate from your life and becomes woven into it.

## What Life Looks Like When Your Nervous System Feels Safe

You're in a meeting and someone criticizes your idea. Your chest tightens, heat rises in your face. Then something different happens. You notice it. You take a breath. The tightness doesn't spiral. It just is. And then it passes.

Living regulated isn't work anymore. It's who you're becoming.

You don't analyze ease. You feel it, in breath, in posture, in the quiet space between thoughts. Your face doesn't hold constant tension. You can make eye contact without your system screaming danger. These aren't dramatic transformations. They're quiet recalibrations that happen over time, teaching your body it doesn't have to be on guard every moment.

Changes appear in unexpected places. You sit in a restaurant without scanning every exit. You receive a compliment without immediately deflecting. You disagree with someone without your throat closing. You rest without guilt eating at you.

Your relationships shift. When your system isn't constantly in threat mode, you stop reacting to people as if they're dangers to manage. You can hear criticism without collapsing into shame. You can express needs without apologizing. You can be close to someone without losing yourself or pushing them away to protect yourself.

Presence becomes more common. Not constant, no one is present all the time. But more often, you're actually in the moment you're in instead of somewhere else in your head. You taste your food. You hear what people say instead of waiting for your turn to talk. You notice the light through the window, the texture of fabric against your skin, the sound of your own breath.

Safety feels like moving freely where armor once lived.

Your capacity has expanded. More life fits inside you now.

Some days will still be hard. You'll still get triggered. Old reflexes still appear, but they no longer define you. The difference is how gently you return.

Your body remembers the milestones even when your mind forgets the effort.

### EXERCISE: Before and After Reflection

This exercise helps you name the changes that have happened through your healing work. Survival patterns focus on what's still wrong, still hurting, still unfinished. This interrupts that and asks you to witness your own progress.

**Before this work, I:**

Felt in my body:

________________________________________________________________________________

________________________________________________________________________________

________________________________________________________________________________

Responded to stress by:

________________________________________________________________________________

________________________________________________________________________________

________________________________________________________________________________

Believed about myself:

________________________________________________________________________________

________________________________________________________________________________

________________________________________________________________________________

**Now, I:**

Feel in my body:

---

---

---

Respond to stress by:

---

---

---

Believe about myself:

---

---

---

One specific moment that shows me something has changed:

---

---

---

## Maintaining Your Healing in Relationships and at Work

Your steadiness doesn't exist in a vacuum. You live in relationship with other people, and their nervous systems interact with yours constantly. Every conversation, every shared space, every exchange of energy involves your system reading theirs and responding.

This is how we're wired. Mirror neurons fire when we observe someone else's emotional state, creating resonance in our own bodies. When someone walks into a room anxious, you feel it. When someone is calm and grounded, that steadiness can help regulate you. This is co-regulation, the way nervous systems influence each other.

For most of your life, this probably felt like a liability. You absorbed other people's stress, anger, anxiety. You couldn't tell where their feelings ended and yours began. Being around dysregulated people left you dysregulated, sometimes for hours or days.

Now you're learning something different: you can be with someone else's dysregulation without taking it into your body. You can stay grounded in your own system while they're in theirs. This doesn't mean you become cold or disconnected. It means you can be present and compassionate without abandoning yourself.

The practice is differentiation. Noticing when your body starts to mirror someone else's state and making a conscious choice about whether to continue matching them or to stay in your own experience. Sometimes matching serves you, when you're comforting a child or supporting someone through grief, co-regulation helps. Other times, matching pulls you into dysregulation that doesn't serve anyone.

You can sense the difference in your body. When healthy co-regulation happens, you feel connected and present. When unhealthy merging happens, you feel invaded, overwhelmed, lost. Pay attention to that distinction.

In the noise of meetings or messages, you can stay steady. Your breath a quiet metronome beneath the rush.

This often means people calm down around you. Coherence is contagious. When you stay steady, you offer your nervous system as a resource for others to borrow stability from. You become a grounding presence without trying, just by maintaining your own state.

Boundaries become clearer when you understand nervous system dynamics. You're not setting boundaries because you're rejecting people or being selfish. You're protecting your balance because that's what allows you to show up as your best self. A depleted, dysregulated you helps no one.

Some relationships will challenge this. People who are used to you absorbing their emotions might resist when you stop. They might push harder, demanding you return to old patterns of over-functioning or caretaking. This is where your commitment to your own nervous system health gets tested.

You can care about someone and still say no. You can love someone and not take on their problems. You can be empathetic without being enmeshed. These aren't contradictions, they're the foundation of sustainable relationship.

Sometimes you'll need to communicate what you're doing. Not defending it or explaining in detail, just naming it clearly: "I need to take a break from this conversation. I can come back to it tomorrow." Or "I notice I'm getting overwhelmed. I'm going to step outside for a few minutes." Or "I can't take this on right now. Let's find another solution."

Direct communication without apology protects both your steadiness and the relationship's integrity. People might not understand at first. That's okay. You're not asking permission to take care of your nervous system, you're informing them that you are.

Watch for the signs that someone or something is dysregulating you. Your breath gets shallow. Your jaw clenches. Your stomach knots. Your mind races or goes blank. These are your system's signals that something isn't safe for you right now. Trust them. Respond to them. Remove yourself if needed, use what you know, do what you need to come back to yourself.

Equally important: notice who and what co-regulates you. The friend whose presence helps you breathe deeper. The colleague whose calm energy steadies you. The environments that let your nervous system relax. Seek these out intentionally. Balance isn't just about managing the hard stuff, it's about actively creating conditions that support your system's health.

---

### EXERCISE: Relational Nervous System Map

---

This exercise helps you identify which relationships and situations support your balance and which challenge it, so you can make intentional choices about your time and energy.

**People or situations that dysregulate me:**

People / Situation________________________________________________

What happens in my body: ________________________________________

People / Situation________________________________________________

What happens in my body: ________________________________________

People / Situation________________________________________________

What happens in my body: ________________________________________

**People or situations that co-regulate me:**

People / Situation________________________________________________

What happens in my body: ________________________________________

People / Situation________________________________________________

What happens in my body: ________________________________________

People / Situation________________________________________________

What happens in my body: ________________________________________

**Boundaries I need to maintain my balance:**

With whom: ______________________________________________________________________

Specific boundary: ________________________________________________________________

With whom: ______________________________________________________________________

Specific boundary: ________________________________________________________________

With whom: ______________________________________________________________________

Specific boundary: ________________________________________________________________

**What I'll use when triggered in relationships:**

When I notice dysregulation starting, I will:

_____________________________________________________________________________

_____________________________________________________________________________

_____________________________________________________________________________

*Review this map monthly. Your nervous system's needs change as you heal, and relationships shift. What dysregulated you six months ago might not affect you the same way now.*

## Knowing When to Seek Additional Support

This workbook has given you understanding and ways to work with trauma held in your body. You've done real work, work that many people never have the courage to begin. But self-guided healing has limits, and recognizing those limits is part of taking care of yourself.

Some trauma is too big to process alone. Some pain needs another person to witness it, hold space for it, help you move through it safely. A book can teach you about your nervous system, but it can't sit with you when you're in the middle of a flashback and can't find your way out. It can't help you work through complex trauma patterns that need professional guidance to unravel.

Needing a therapist isn't failure. It's the next level of commitment to your healing. The understanding you've gained here will serve you in therapy, you'll know what's happening in your body, you'll have language for your experiences, you'll be able to work with a therapist more effectively because you've built this foundation. But sometimes you need someone trained to go deeper with you.

Consider professional support if you notice these signs: Your symptoms interfere with your ability to function in daily life. You can't work, maintain relationships, or care for yourself in basic ways because of trauma responses. What you've learned helps some, but not enough to get you through the day.

Trauma memories overwhelm you frequently. You're having flashbacks, intrusive thoughts, or dissociative episodes that you can't manage with the techniques in this book. The past feels more real than the present more often than not.

You're experiencing self-harm urges or suicidal thoughts. This is non-negotiable. These thoughts mean your pain has reached a level that requires immediate professional intervention. Call a crisis line, go to an emergency room, tell someone you trust. You don't have to handle this alone, and you shouldn't.

What you've learned works temporarily but the dysregulation returns quickly. You can find balance in the moment, but the underlying patterns stay stuck. You need someone who can help you work with the deeper layers that self-guided work can't reach.

You want someone to witness your healing. Sometimes the act of being seen, heard, and validated by another person is what allows trauma to fully release. A book can give you understanding; a therapist can give you relationship, and relationship is where much of our trauma occurred and where much of our healing happens.

Finding the right therapist matters. Not every therapist understands trauma, and not every trauma therapist works somatically. You want someone who gets that healing happens in the body, not just through talking about the body.

Look for therapists trained in somatic approaches: Somatic Experiencing, Sensorimotor Psychotherapy, somatic-based IFS, EMDR, or other body-centered modalities. Ask potential therapists directly: "How do you work with trauma stored in the body?" Listen to their answer. If they only talk about thoughts and behaviors, keep looking.

You want someone who understands Complex Post-Traumatic Stress Disorder (Complex PTSD) if that's your experience. Developmental trauma, attachment wounds, and chronic relational trauma require different approaches than single-incident trauma. Make sure your therapist has specific training in complex trauma.

Ask about their approach to parts work if that's been helpful for you through this book. Many somatic therapists integrate Internal Family Systems or similar frameworks. If working with your parts has opened something for you, find someone who can go deeper into that territory with you.

Trust your nervous system when you meet with potential therapists. Do you feel safe with this person? Does your body relax slightly or does it tense up? Therapy only works if your nervous system can settle enough to do the work. If something feels off, that's information. You don't owe anyone your business. Keep looking.

Some therapists offer free consultation calls. Use these to ask questions: What's your experience with Complex PTSD? How do you approach somatic healing? What does a typical session look like? How do you handle it when clients get activated or dissociate? The right therapist will answer these questions directly and warmly, without jargon or defensiveness.

Cost is real. Therapy is expensive, and not everyone has access. If money is a barrier, look for therapists who offer sliding scale fees, community mental health centers, training clinics where graduate students see clients at reduced rates under supervision, or online platforms that cost less than traditional therapy. Some workplaces offer Employee Assistance Programs with free sessions. Some therapists reserve a few spots for pro bono clients. Ask. Advocate for yourself. Your healing matters.

Group therapy or support groups can be powerful and more affordable. Being with others who understand what you've survived, who see your pain and reflect back that you're not alone, this can be profoundly healing. Look for trauma-specific groups, either in person or online.

Remember that starting therapy doesn't mean the work you've done here was insufficient. It means you're continuing your healing journey with additional support. Every bit of awareness you've gained, every moment of reconnection with your body, all of that comes with you into therapy and makes the work more effective.

---

### EXERCISE: Assessing My Support Needs

---

Use this exercise to honestly evaluate whether you'd benefit from professional support right now. There's no shame in any answer, just information about what you need.

**I've made progress in:**

______________________________________________________________________

______________________________________________________________________

______________________________________________________________________

______________________________________________________________________

**I'm still struggling with:**

______________________________________________________________________

______________________________________________________________________

______________________________________________________________________

______________________________________________________________________

**Signs I might benefit from professional support:**

☐ Symptoms interfere with daily life (work, relationships, basic self-care)

☐ Trauma memories or flashbacks overwhelm me regularly

☐ I'm experiencing self-harm urges or suicidal thoughts

☐ I can find balance in the moment but dysregulation returns quickly

☐ I want someone to witness and support my healing process

☐ I've reached the limits of what I can process alone

☐ I need help with specific trauma that feels too big to face by myself

**If I checked any boxes above, my next step is:**

Within the next week, I will:

_______________________________________________________________________________

_______________________________________________________________________________

Within the next month, I will:

_______________________________________________________________________________

_______________________________________________________________________________

**Resources I can use to find support:**

• Therapist directories: _______________________________________________________

• Insurance provider list: _____________________________________________________

• Referrals from: ____________________________________________________________

• Crisis support (if needed): __________________________________________________

*Note: Keep this page accessible. Revisit it if your symptoms change or intensify.*

## Honoring How Far You've Come

Pause here. Before moving forward, before thinking about what's next, stop and look back at where you started.

You picked up this workbook because something in you knew you needed to heal. Maybe you were desperate. Maybe you were curious. Maybe you'd tried everything else and nothing had worked. Whatever brought you here, you showed up. That took courage.

You learned that trauma isn't just in your mind, it's in your tissues, your nervous system, your breath, your posture, your gut. You learned that the symptoms you've lived with aren't character flaws or signs that you're broken. They're your body's intelligent responses to overwhelming experiences, survival strategies that once kept you safe.

You've met the fragments of yourself that once fought for control, and you've learned to let them rest inside one steady rhythm.

You worked with emotions and memories trapped in your body. You learned techniques for releasing what's been locked inside, for moving through stuck activation, for completing self-protective responses that got interrupted during trauma. Your body started trusting that it could let go because you were finally giving it ways to do so.

Maybe you addressed chronic pain and discovered that some of what you thought was purely physical had roots in unprocessed trauma. Maybe you worked with dissociation and found ways to anchor yourself when you float away. Maybe you learned to find grounding until it started feeling less like a technique and more like a way of being.

Look at the specific changes. You might notice your body's signals earlier now. You might be able to stay present during conflict instead of disappearing inside yourself. You might feel your feelings without being destroyed by them, or set boundaries you couldn't have imagined setting before.

These changes aren't dramatic movie moments. They're quiet, cumulative, daily shifts that add up to a different relationship with yourself and your body. They're the kind of progress that's easy to overlook because it happens gradually, but that doesn't make it any less real or significant.

You did this work when it would have been easier to stay numb. When it would have been safer to keep avoiding your body. When it would have been less painful to maintain the status quo. You chose growth over comfort, healing over familiarity, possibility over resignation.

That matters. It matters that you showed up page after page, exercise after exercise, even when it was hard. It matters that you were honest with yourself about your pain, your patterns, your fears. It matters that you tried approaches even when you weren't sure they'd work. It matters that you kept going.

Some of you will minimize this. Old patterns will want to focus on what's not fixed yet, what still hurts, what you haven't achieved. That's what survival patterns do, they scan for threat, for inadequacy, for proof that you're still not okay. But right now, in this moment, interrupt that pattern. Look at what is different. Acknowledge what you've learned and integrated. Let yourself see your own strength.

This isn't arrogance or self-congratulation. It's recognition. It's bearing witness to your own transformation, however incomplete it might feel. What we don't acknowledge, we don't fully own. And you've earned the right to own this healing.

A simple way to honor this journey: whisper thank you to the body that carried you here.

---

### ✏ EXERCISE: My Healing Journey Letter

---

Write a letter to yourself acknowledging the work you've done. This isn't about being fully healed, it's about recognizing the journey you've taken and the courage it required.

Dear ____________________________________,

When you started this workbook, you were feeling:

______________________________________________________________________________

______________________________________________________________________________

______________________________________________________________________________

______________________________________________________________________________

The bravest thing you did was:

______________________________________________________________________________

______________________________________________________________________________

______________________________________________________________________________

______________________________________________________________________________

You learned that your body:

______________________________________________________________________________

______________________________________________________________________________

______________________________________________________________________________

______________________________________________________________________________

What helped you most was:

______________________________________________________________________________

______________________________________________________________________________

______________________________________________________________________________

______________________________________________________________________________

The biggest shift you've noticed is:

______________________________________________________________________________

______________________________________________________________________________

______________________________________________________________________________

______________________________________________________________________________

I want you to know:

________________________________________________________________________________

________________________________________________________________________________

________________________________________________________________________________

________________________________________________________________________________

As you continue forward, remember:

________________________________________________________________________________

________________________________________________________________________________

________________________________________________________________________________

________________________________________________________________________________

With compassion,

______________________________

*After writing this letter, read it aloud to yourself. Let your body hear these words. Save this letter somewhere you can return to it during difficult times when you need a reminder of how far you've come.*

## Your Body as Your Greatest Ally Moving Forward

You started this workbook seeing your body as a problem to solve. A place where bad things happened and got stuck. A battlefield where symptoms raged and you fought daily just to function. Your body felt like the enemy, betraying you with panic attacks, dissociation, pain, numbness, hypervigilance.

What if that's not what happened at all?

Every reaction your body learned was protection. Every symptom was a signal of love, not failure.

Your body remembered what your mind couldn't bear, holding the story until you were ready to hear it. It created symptoms because it needed you to pay attention. It kept you alive through things that could have destroyed you. It has been working for you all along.

Now you're learning to work with your body instead of against it. To listen to its signals as information rather than dismiss them as problems. To respond to its needs with curiosity and compassion instead of frustration or control.

This relationship isn't maintenance anymore. It's instinct.

Every day, you'll have opportunities to tune in or tune out. To honor what your body is telling you or override it. To treat yourself with care or push through regardless of what you're feeling.

Now you can answer back. Not with analysis, but with presence.

Some days will be easier than others. You'll have moments when you slip back into old patterns, pushing, ignoring, numbing, controlling. That's human. Return becomes familiar.

Your body speaks in a hundred dialects of sensation. Pressure, warmth, tremor, release. These aren't just random physical experiences, they're your body's language, constantly communicating about your internal state, your environment, your needs.

The more you listen, the more fluent you become. You start noticing subtle shifts earlier. You catch the first signs of dysregulation before it escalates. You feel the difference between anxiety and excitement, between grief and depression, between healthy rest and dissociative collapse. These distinctions help you respond appropriately instead of treating every uncomfortable sensation as an emergency.

Your body also offers you pleasure, joy, aliveness. Not just after you've "fixed" everything, but right now, in the middle of healing. The warmth of sun on your skin. The satisfaction of a deep stretch. The comfort of a soft blanket. The taste of food you actually enjoy. The feeling of your feet on the ground. These aren't trivial experiences, they're your nervous system learning that being in your body can feel good, that sensation isn't only about pain and threat.

Moving forward, commit to what keeps you connected to your body. Not because you have to, but because you want to live in partnership with this body that's carried you through everything. Choose three approaches from this workbook that resonated most and make them part of your rhythm. Maybe it's morning body scans, grounding through your feet, pendulation when you're overwhelmed. Whatever works for you, keep doing it.

Your body will continue teaching you if you keep listening. It will show you what you need, warn you when something isn't right, guide you toward what helps you thrive. Trust it. Not blindly, trauma can make your threat detection overly sensitive, and you'll need to discern between real danger and triggered responses. But trust that your body is giving you information worth paying attention to.

You're not just managing trauma anymore. You're building a life where your nervous system feels safe more often than not. Where your body feels like home instead of a war zone. Where you can be fully present for the life you're living instead of just surviving it.

### EXERCISE: Body Gratitude and Commitment Practice

This closing exercise creates a conscious partnership between you and your body going forward. Use it as a ritual to seal your commitment to continuing this work.

Find a quiet space. Place one hand on your heart and one on your belly. Take three slow breaths, feeling your hands rise and fall.

**I thank my body for:**

Surviving what felt unsurvivable:

_______________________________________________

_______________________________________________

Carrying me this far:

_______________________________________________

_______________________________________________

Specific ways my body has protected or served me:

_______________________________________________

_______________________________________________

**I commit to my body:**

- Listening when it speaks instead of ignoring its signals
- Responding to its needs with compassion instead of judgment

Continuing these specific approaches:

- ____________________
- ____________________
- ____________________
- ____________________
- ____________________
- ____________________

Trusting its wisdom as I move forward

**My body's message to me right now:**

Place both hands on your heart. Close your eyes. Breathe. Listen. Write whatever words, feelings, or knowing arises:

_______________________________________________

_______________________________________________

_______________________________________________

_______________________________________________

Now, speak these words aloud. Feel them in your body as you say them. Let your nervous system register this commitment. Return to this gesture whenever you need to reconnect with your body or remember your commitment to living in partnership with it. Your body has always been on your side. Now you listen when it speaks, move when it whispers, rest when it softens. Together, you return, not to healing, but to living.

# Your Experience Can Light Someone's Path

*"We heal in connection. What we share helps others find their way." — Unknown*

Would you help someone you've never met if it cost nothing and took less than a minute?

Someone you'll likely never know is searching right now, confused about why their body won't relax, desperate to understand their nervous system but unsure where to turn. This is where you come in.

If this workbook has been valuable, would you take a moment to leave an honest review? It costs nothing and takes less than 60 seconds.

I appreciate all reviews, whether positive or negative, and I will read them personally. Your honest words help:

- One more person discover body-based trauma healing
- One more nervous system begin regulation
- One more life move toward safety

Thank you from my heart.

# References

---

## Chapter 1: Your Body Holds the Story Your Mind Forgot

---


Levine, P. A. (1997). *Waking the tiger: Healing trauma.* North Atlantic Books.

Levine, P. A. (2010). *In an unspoken voice: How the body releases trauma and restores goodness.* North Atlantic Books.

Ogden, P., Minton, K., & Pain, C. (2006). *Trauma and the body: A sensorimotor approach to psychotherapy.* W. W. Norton & Company.

Porges, S. W. (2011). *The polyvagal theory: Neurophysiological foundations of emotions, attachment, communication, and self-regulation.* W. W. Norton & Company.

Schore, A. N. (2003). *Affect regulation and the repair of the self.* W. W. Norton & Company.

Siegel, D. J. (2012). *The developing mind: How relationships and the brain interact to shape who we are* (2nd ed.). Guilford Press.

van der Kolk, B. A. (2014). *The body keeps the score: Brain, mind, and body in the healing of trauma.* Viking.


---

## Chapter 2: Meeting Your Nervous System

---


Dana, D. (2018). *The polyvagal theory in therapy: Engaging the rhythm of regulation.* W. W. Norton & Company.

Levine, P. A. (1997). *Waking the tiger: Healing trauma.* North Atlantic Books.

Ogden, P., Minton, K., & Pain, C. (2006). *Trauma and the body: A sensorimotor approach to psychotherapy.* W. W. Norton & Company.

Porges, S. W. (2011). *The polyvagal theory: Neurophysiological foundations of emotions, attachment, communication, and self-regulation.* W. W. Norton & Company.

Porges, S. W. (2017). *The pocket guide to the polyvagal theory: The transformative power of feeling safe.* W. W. Norton & Company.

Rothschild, B. (2000). *The body remembers: The psychophysiology of trauma and trauma treatment.* W. W. Norton & Company.

van der Kolk, B. A. (2014). *The body keeps the score: Brain, mind, and body in the healing of trauma.* Viking.

Walker, P. (2013). *Complex PTSD: From surviving to thriving*. Azure Coyote.

---

## Chapter 3: Learning to Feel Safe in Your Own Skin

Dana, D. (2018). *The polyvagal theory in therapy: Engaging the rhythm of regulation*. W. W. Norton & Company.

Dana, D. (2020). *Polyvagal exercises for safety and connection: 50 client-centered practices*. W. W. Norton & Company.

Levine, P. A. (2010). *In an unspoken voice: How the body releases trauma and restores goodness*. North Atlantic Books.

Ogden, P., & Fisher, J. (2015). *Sensorimotor psychotherapy: Interventions for trauma and attachment*. W. W. Norton & Company.

Porges, S. W. (2011). *The polyvagal theory: Neurophysiological foundations of emotions, attachment, communication, and self-regulation*. W. W. Norton & Company.

Siegel, D. J. (1999). *The developing mind: How relationships and the brain interact to shape who we are*. Guilford Press.

Schore, A. N. (2003). *Affect dysregulation and disorders of the self*. W. W. Norton & Company.

van der Kolk, B. A. (2014). *The body keeps the score: Brain, mind, and body in the healing of trauma*. Viking.

---

----

## Chapter 4: Befriending Your Body Again

---

Gendlin, E. T. (1982). *Focusing*. Bantam Books.

Levine, P. A. (1997). *Waking the tiger: Healing trauma*. North Atlantic Books.

Levine, P. A. (2010). *In an unspoken voice: How the body releases trauma and restores goodness*. North Atlantic Books.

Ogden, P., Minton, K., & Pain, C. (2006). *Trauma and the body: A sensorimotor approach to psychotherapy*. W. W. Norton & Company.

Ogden, P., & Fisher, J. (2015). *Sensorimotor psychotherapy: Interventions for trauma and attachment*. W. W. Norton & Company.

Payne, P., Levine, P. A., & Crane-Godreau, M. A. (2015). Somatic experiencing: Using interoception and proprioception as core elements of trauma therapy. *Frontiers in Psychology*, *6*, 93.

Price, C. J., & Hooven, C. (2018). Interoceptive awareness skills for emotion regulation: Theory and approach of mindful awareness in body-oriented therapy (MABT). *Frontiers in Psychology*, 9, 798.

van der Kolk, B. A. (2014). *The body keeps the score: Brain, mind, and body in the healing of trauma*. Viking.

---------------------------------------------------------------------------------------

----

**Chapter 5: Understanding Dissociation and Coming Back Home**

---------------------------------------------------------------------------------------

Fisher, J. (2017). *Healing the fragmented selves of trauma survivors: Overcoming internal self-alienation*. Routledge.

Lanius, R. A., Vermetten, E., & Pain, C. (Eds.). (2010). *The impact of early life trauma on health and disease: The hidden epidemic*. Cambridge University Press.

Levine, P. A. (2010). *In an unspoken voice: How the body releases trauma and restores goodness*. North Atlantic Books.

Nijenhuis, E. R. S., & van der Hart, O. (2011). Dissociation in trauma: A new definition and comparison with previous formulations. *Journal of Trauma & Dissociation, 12*(4), 416-445.

Ogden, P., & Fisher, J. (2015). *Sensorimotor psychotherapy: Interventions for trauma and attachment*. W. W. Norton & Company.

Porges, S. W. (2011). *The polyvagal theory: Neurophysiological foundations of emotions, attachment, communication, and self-regulation*. W. W. Norton & Company.

Schauer, M., & Elbert, T. (2010). Dissociation following traumatic stress: Etiology and treatment. *Zeitschrift für Psychologie/Journal of Psychology, 218*(2), 109-127.

Steele, K., van der Hart, O., & Nijenhuis, E. R. S. (2005). Phase-oriented treatment of structural dissociation in complex traumatization: Overcoming trauma-related phobias. *Journal of Trauma & Dissociation, 6*(3), 11-53.

van der Kolk, B. A. (2014). *The body keeps the score: Brain, mind, and body in the healing of trauma*. Viking.

---------------------------------------------------------------------------------------

**Chapter 6: Releasing Suppressed Emotions Trapped in Your Tissues**

---------------------------------------------------------------------------------------

Damasio, A. (1999). *The feeling of what happens: Body and emotion in the making of consciousness*. Harcourt.

Levine, P. A. (1997). *Waking the tiger: Healing trauma*. North Atlantic Books.

Levine, P. A. (2010). *In an unspoken voice: How the body releases trauma and restores goodness*. North Atlantic Books.

Ogden, P., Minton, K., & Pain, C. (2006). *Trauma and the body: A sensorimotor approach to psychotherapy*. W. W. Norton & Company.

Pert, C. B. (1997). *Molecules of emotion: Why you feel the way you feel*. Scribner.

Rosenberg, S. (2017). *Accessing the healing power of the vagus nerve: Self-help exercises for anxiety, depression, trauma, and autism*. North Atlantic Books.

Scaer, R. C. (2014). *The body bears the burden: Trauma, dissociation, and disease* (3rd ed.). Routledge.

van der Kolk, B. A. (2014). *The body keeps the score: Brain, mind, and body in the healing of trauma*. Viking.

---

**Chapter 7: Feeling Away Your Chronic Pain and Illness**

---

Gatchel, R. J., Peng, Y. B., Peters, M. L., Fuchs, P. N., & Turk, D. C. (2007). The biopsychosocial approach to chronic pain: Scientific advances and future directions. *Psychological Bulletin, 133*(4), 581-624.

Gordon, A., & Ziv, A. (2021). *The way out: A revolutionary, scientifically proven approach to healing chronic pain*. Avery.

Levine, P. A. (2010). *In an unspoken voice: How the body releases trauma and restores goodness*. North Atlantic Books.

Moseley, G. L., & Butler, D. S. (2015). *Explain pain* (2nd ed.). Noigroup Publications.

Schubiner, H., & Betzold, M. (2016). *Unlearn your pain: A 28-day process to reprogram your brain* (3rd ed.). Mind Body Publishing.

Sarno, J. E. (1991). *Healing back pain: The mind-body connection*. Warner Books.

van der Kolk, B. A. (2014). *The body keeps the score: Brain, mind, and body in the healing of trauma*. Viking.

Wager, T. D., Atlas, L. Y., Lindquist, M. A., Roy, M., Woo, C. W., & Kross, E. (2013). An fMRI-based neurologic signature of physical pain. *New England Journal of Medicine, 368*(15), 1388-1397.

---

**Chapter 8: Meeting Your Inner Parts Through IFS**

---

Anderson, F. G., Sweezy, M., & Schwartz, R. C. (2017). *Internal Family Systems skills training manual: Trauma-informed treatment for anxiety, depression, PTSD & substance abuse*. PESI Publishing & Media.

Fisher, J. (2017). *Healing the fragmented selves of trauma survivors: Overcoming internal self-alienation*. Routledge.

Schwartz, R. C. (1995). *Internal Family Systems therapy*. Guilford Press.

Schwartz, R. C. (2001). *Introduction to the Internal Family Systems model.* Trailheads Publications.

Schwartz, R. C., & Sweezy, M. (2020). *Internal Family Systems therapy* (2nd ed.). Guilford Press.

Sinason, V. (Ed.). (2002). *Attachment, trauma and multiplicity: Working with dissociative identity disorder.* Routledge.

Siegel, D. J. (2010). *Mindsight: The new science of personal transformation.* Bantam Books.

van der Kolk, B. A. (2014). *The body keeps the score: Brain, mind, and body in the healing of trauma.* Viking.

--------------------------------------------------------------------------------
----

**Chapter 9: Stop Anxiety Attacks Before They Take Over**

--------------------------------------------------------------------------------

Bourne, E. J. (2015). *The anxiety and phobia workbook* (6th ed.). New Harbinger Publications.

Brown, B. (2012). *Daring greatly: How the courage to be vulnerable transforms the way we live, love, parent, and lead.* Gotham Books.

Clark, D. M. (1986). A cognitive approach to panic. *Behaviour Research and Therapy, 24*(4), 461-470.

Dana, D. (2018). *The polyvagal theory in therapy: Engaging the rhythm of regulation.* W. W. Norton & Company.

Levine, P. A. (2010). *In an unspoken voice: How the body releases trauma and restores goodness.* North Atlantic Books.

Neff, K. (2011). *Self-compassion: The proven power of being kind to yourself.* William Morrow.

Ogden, P., & Fisher, J. (2015). *Sensorimotor psychotherapy: Interventions for trauma and attachment.* W. W. Norton & Company.

Porges, S. W. (2011). *The polyvagal theory: Neurophysiological foundations of emotions, attachment, communication, and self-regulation.* W. W. Norton & Company.

van der Kolk, B. A. (2014). *The body keeps the score: Brain, mind, and body in the healing of trauma.* Viking.

--------------------------------------------------------------------------------
----

**Chapter 10: Healing Depression Through the Body**

--------------------------------------------------------------------------------

Cuddy, A. (2015). *Presence: Bringing your boldest self to your most challenging moments.* Little, Brown and Company.

Dana, D. (2018). *The polyvagal theory in therapy: Engaging the rhythm of regulation.* W. W. Norton &

Company.

Kabat-Zinn, J. (1990). *Full catastrophe living: Using the wisdom of your body and mind to face stress, pain, and illness.* Delacorte Press.

Levine, P. A. (2010). *In an unspoken voice: How the body releases trauma and restores goodness.* North Atlantic Books.

Martell, C. R., Dimidjian, S., & Herman-Dunn, R. (2010). *Behavioral activation for depression: A clinician's guide.* Guilford Press.

Ogden, P., Minton, K., & Pain, C. (2006). *Trauma and the body: A sensorimotor approach to psychotherapy.* W. W. Norton & Company.

Porges, S. W. (2011). *The polyvagal theory: Neurophysiological foundations of emotions, attachment, communication, and self-regulation.* W. W. Norton & Company.

Ratey, J. J., & Hagerman, E. (2008). *Spark: The revolutionary new science of exercise and the brain.* Little, Brown and Company.

van der Kolk, B. A. (2014). *The body keeps the score: Brain, mind, and body in the healing of trauma.* Viking.

---

**Chapter 11: Somatic Tools for Daily Nervous System Regulation**

---

Csikszentmihalyi, M. (1990). *Flow: The psychology of optimal experience.* Harper & Row.

Dana, D. (2020). *Polyvagal exercises for safety and connection: 50 client-centered practices.* W. W. Norton & Company.

Gendlin, E. T. (1982). *Focusing.* Bantam Books.

Kabat-Zinn, J. (1994). *Wherever you go, there you are: Mindfulness meditation in everyday life.* Hyperion.

Levine, P. A. (2010). *In an unspoken voice: How the body releases trauma and restores goodness.* North Atlantic Books.

Ogden, P., & Fisher, J. (2015). *Sensorimotor psychotherapy: Interventions for trauma and attachment.* W. W. Norton & Company.

Porges, S. W. (2017). *The pocket guide to the polyvagal theory: The transformative power of feeling safe.* W. W. Norton & Company.

Rosenberg, S. (2017). *Accessing the healing power of the vagus nerve: Self-help exercises for anxiety, depression, trauma, and autism.* North Atlantic Books.

Siegel, D. J. (2007). *The mindful brain: Reflection and attunement in the cultivation of well-being.* W. W.

Norton & Company.

---

____**Chapter 12: Living in a Regulated Body**

---

Dana, D. (2018). *The polyvagal theory in therapy: Engaging the rhythm of regulation*. W. W. Norton & Company.

Hanson, R. (2013). *Hardwiring happiness: The new brain science of contentment, calm, and confidence*. Harmony Books.

Levine, P. A. (2010). *In an unspoken voice: How the body releases trauma and restores goodness*. North Atlantic Books.

Porges, S. W. (2011). *The polyvagal theory: Neurophysiological foundations of emotions, attachment, communication, and self-regulation*. W. W. Norton & Company.

Schwartz, R. C., & Sweezy, M. (2020). *Internal Family Systems therapy* (2nd ed.). Guilford Press.

Siegel, D. J. (2010). *Mindsight: The new science of personal transformation*. Bantam Books.

Siegel, D. J. (2012). *The developing mind: How relationships and the brain interact to shape who we are* (2nd ed.). Guilford Press.

van der Kolk, B. A. (2014). *The body keeps the score: Brain, mind, and body in the healing of trauma*. Viking.

Walker, P. (2013). *Complex PTSD: From surviving to thriving*. Azure Coyote.

www.ingramcontent.com/pod-product-compliance
Ingram Content Group UK Ltd.
Pitfield, Milton Keynes, MK11 3LW, UK
UKHW050950290926
15470UKWH00005B/1747

9 781806 472321